World Bank Discussion Papers

Women in Higher Education

Progress, Constraints, and Promising Initiatives

K. Subbarao
Laura Raney
Halil Dundar
Jennifer Haworth

The World Bank
Washington, D.C.

NS
2/16/95

Copyright © 1994
The International Bank for Reconstruction
and Development/THE WORLD BANK
1818 H Street, N.W.
Washington, D.C. 20433, U.S.A.

Discussion Papers present results of country analysis or research that are circulated to encourage discussion and comment within the development community. To present these results with the least possible delay, the typescript of this paper has not been prepared in accordance with the procedures appropriate to formal printed texts, and the World Bank accepts no responsibility for errors. Some sources cited in this paper may be informal documents that are not readily available.

The findings, interpretations, and conclusions expressed in this paper are entirely those of the author(s) and should not be attributed in any manner to the World Bank, to its affiliated organizations, or to members of its Board of Executive Directors or the countries they represent. The World Bank does not guarantee the accuracy of the data included in this publication and accepts no responsibility whatsoever for any consequence of their use. The boundaries, colors, denominations, and other information shown on any map in this volume do not imply on the part of the World Bank Group any judgment on the legal status of any territory or the endorsement or acceptance of such boundaries.

The material in this publication is copyrighted. Requests for permission to reproduce portions of it should be sent to the Office of the Publisher at the address shown in the copyright notice above. The World Bank encourages dissemination of its work and will normally give permission promptly and, when the reproduction is for noncommercial purposes, without asking a fee. Permission to copy portions for classroom use is granted through the Copyright Clearance Center, Inc., Suite 910, 222 Rosewood Drive, Danvers, Massachusetts 01923, U.S.A.

The complete backlist of publications from the World Bank is shown in the annual *Index of Publications,* which contains an alphabetical title list (with full ordering information) and indexes of subjects, authors, and countries and regions. The latest edition is available free of charge from the Distribution Unit, Office of the Publisher, The World Bank, 1818 H Street, N.W., Washington, D.C. 20433, U.S.A., or from Publications, The World Bank, 66, avenue d'Iéna, 75116 Paris, France.

ISSN: 0259-210X

K. Subbarao is a senior economist in the World Bank's Education and Social Policy Department. Laura Raney was a consultant and Halil Dundar and Jennifer Haworth were summer interns in the Department.

Library of Congress Cataloging-in-Publication Data

Women in higher education : progress, constraints, and promising
    initiatives / K. Subbarao ... [et al.].
        p.   cm. — (World Bank discussion papers ; 244)
    Includes bibliographical references.
    ISBN 0-8213-2859-X
    1. Women—Education, Higher—Developing countries. 2. Women
college students—Developing countries. 3. College attendance—
Developing countries.   I. Subbarao, K.   II. Series.
LC2572.W66   1994
376'.65'091724—dc20   94-16695
                                                CIP

Contents

Tables

Figures

Boxes

FOREWORD

Many studies have shown that the economic and social returns to female education at all levels are considerable. A few recent studies have also analyzed the gender gap in primary and secondary schooling. However, practically no comprehensive analysis of the gender gap in higher education is currently available. This paper fills this gap. The paper examines the trends in women's access and achievement in higher education, including student enrollment patterns in various fields and women's access to faculty and administrative positions. Based on the Bank's project experience, the paper also identifies some of the more successful strategies and measures to reduce the gender gap in higher education.

K. Y. Amoako
Director
Education and Social Policy Department

ABSTRACT

Improving and widening access to education has been a major goal in most developing countries in the past three decades. Impressive progress has been achieved at all levels. Two issues are examined in this paper. First, how did women fare in the wake of this general expansion of tertiary enrollments? (Part I) Second, what programs and policies contributed to enhancing women's enrollment in the context of World Bank project experience? (Part II)

Part I shows that despite the potential of women's higher education to economic growth, a "gender gap" in enrollments at the tertiary level is pervasive, especially in Sub-Saharan Africa, the Middle East, and South Asia. Unlike in the case of primary and secondary enrollments where demand side factors were important, easing the constraints on the supply side was critical in improving the gender parity in higher education.

The gains in female enrollments since the 1970s need to be interpreted with caution since few women were able to make a dent into sciences and engineering. Indeed, gender streaming appeared pervasive in all countries, including developed countries, with women being overrepresented in humanities and vocational schools. Pro-active (incentive) policies are needed both at the secondary school level (to induce girls to opt for sciences and mathematics), and at the university level.

In Part II of this paper, the policies that were explicitly tried to increase women's access were examined with reference to the World Bank's project experience from 1972-92. The severity and extent of constraints varied across regions and countries and a variety of measures have been taken to improve women's access to and achievement in higher education. Results as to what works are limited, and many projects are on-going.

In terms of broad patterns across countries, the reviewed evidence suggests that countries with low per capita income levels <u>and</u> difficult social setting (e.g. India, Pakistan, Nepal, Bangladesh and many countries in Sub-Saharan Africa), may have the greatest barriers to female participation. In such situations, a promising approach is the introduction of multiple components in the projects to overcome an array of social and economic barriers which inhibit female participation in higher education. By contrast, in low income countries with less severe social constraints, expansion of places has itself been generally successful. However, even in these countries, establishing a link between the programs offered and the opportunities for women in the labor market was found to be critical. High secondary enrollment rates, impressive rates of return for women's education, and the availability of student places do not necessarily guarantee an increase in women's participation in higher education -- unless the programs are dovetailed to meet the specific demands of the labor market.

ACKNOWLEDGEMENTS

We are grateful for comments and suggestions of participants of a Bankwide seminar on an earlier version of this paper. We are indebted to William Saint for reviewing the paper with great care and for his constructive comments and suggestions. We also wish to thank Professor Nanak Kakwani for his contribution to the methodology contained in Section 3 of the paper. We are grateful to Benjamin Crow for the production of the paper.

EXECUTIVE SUMMARY

i.   Higher education for women is important not only for equal education opportunities between the sexes, but also because of the substantial economic returns achieved by raising women's productivity and the health, educational and income levels of families. Investments in higher education, particularly in developing countries, have high private rates of return measured by associated wage increases. The prevailing high rates of return are also indicative of the existence of productive opportunities for women.

ii.   Over the last four decades, tertiary enrollments expanded manifold throughout the developing world. New institutions mushroomed, and more places were added to the old institutions. Two issues are examined in this paper. First, how did women fare in the wake of this general expansion of tertiary enrollments? (Part I) Second, what programs and policies contributed to enhancing women's enrollment in the context of World Bank project experience? (Part II)

iii.   Part I shows that despite the potential of women's higher education to economic growth, a "gender gap" in enrollments at the tertiary level is pervasive, especially in Sub-Saharan Africa, the Middle East, and South Asia. This gender disparity implies that a large number of potential candidates are denied the opportunity to participate actively in productive activities and contribute to faster economic development.

iv.   Movements in gender parity in enrollments are largely driven by the initial level of enrollments and the growth rate of enrollments. Thus, unlike in the case of primary and secondary enrollments where demand side factors were important,[1] easing the constraints on the supply side was critical in improving the gender parity in higher education.

v.   A three-factor decomposition analysis showed that while general expansion accounted for about 70 per cent of the change in female enrollments over the 1970s, a change (improvement) in gender parity contributed only about 20-25 per cent. General expansion of tertiary enrollments benefitted women substantially. This finding holds good whether the countries are classified by regions or by per capita income levels. The very high private rates of return to higher education may have been an important factor behind the observed general expansion and consequential favorable impact on female enrollments.

vi.   Of the many factors influencing female tertiary enrollments, two are important: (a) female secondary enrollments, and dropout rates of girls at the secondary level, which together set the limits for female tertiary enrollments; and (b) structural changes such as the expansion of the services sector which may trigger the demand for higher-educated female labor. Owing to the absence of a reliable data base, this paper could not address the issue of dropout rates across countries. Therefore, causality could not be established on what determines the level of female tertiary enrollments. However, simple correlations do suggest that lagged female secondary enrollments and the extent of service sector activity are positively correlated to female tertiary enrollments.

vii.   The gains in female enrollments since the 1970s need to be interpreted with caution since few women were able to make a dent into sciences and engineering. Indeed, gender streaming appeared pervasive in all countries, including the developed countries, with women being overrepresented in humanities and vocational schools. Pro-active (incentive) policies are needed both at the secondary school level (to induce girls to opt for sciences and mathematics), and at the university level.

---

[1] See B.Herz, K. Subbarao, M. Habib and L. Raney, (1991): Letting Girls Learn, World Bank Discussion Paper No.133.

viii.   In Part II of this paper, the policies that were explicitly tried to increase women's access were examined with reference to the World Bank's project experience. Over 253 education projects with higher education components were reviewed. On the basis of the reviewed evidence, some promising approaches to reduce the gender gap in higher education are outlined.

ix.   The Bank's early projects focussed on building infrastructures and developing educational planning capacity. Since the early 1980s, the Bank-assisted projects have introduced policy reforms affecting the expansion, financing and internal efficiency of higher education systems. Thus, despite the persistence of gender disparity in most developing countries, the Bank-assisted projects during 1970-85 rarely mentioned gender disparity as an issue, nor introduced significant policies to overcome it. Since the mid-1980s, however, the situation has changed, and many Bank-assisted projects have begun to pay attention to gender disparity.

x.   The severity and extent of constraints varied across regions/countries. Economic constraints, such as unfavorable labor market situation for women, were the most limiting factors in some countries. In other countries, societal constraints, such as lack of single sex institutions, inadequate supply of female teachers or insufficient dorm facilities, proved to be the strongest barriers to female participation. Identification of constraints for female participation in higher education varied a great deal across the regions. In South Asia and East Asia, such identification preceded project formulation, whereas identification of constraints appeared with less frequency in Sub-Saharan Africa and MENA regions.

xi.   Numerous interventions have been introduced in Bank-assisted projects, including general expansion of student places, reservation of student places for women (e.g. Nepal), expansion of places in traditional fields of study (e.g. in countries in the MENA region), expansion of places in non-traditional (e.g. India), setting up single-sex institutions (e.g. Oman), curriculum reform and modification of admission criteria for women (e.g. the Gambia), provision of scholarships and financial assistance (e.g. Papua New Guinea), expansion of boarding facilities (e.g. India and Yemen), recruitment of female faculty (e.g.Yemen), community awareness campaigns (e.g. Korea), and counselling and guidance (e.g. Korea). Regionally, a wider variety of specific interventions to reduce gender disparity was introduced in East Asia than in other regions.

xii.   Results as to what works are limited, and many projects are on-going. Projects with only a single intervention were successful in societies where the formal labor market is growing and few social constraints or qualifications inhibit women's participation. However, in countries where social factors, including low secondary enrollment rates for women, high direct costs of women's education, and cultural restrictions within the labor market, were pervasive, single interventions are unlikely to succeed.

xiii.   In terms of broad patterns across countries, the reviewed evidence suggests that countries with low per capita income levels and difficult social setting (e.g. India, Pakistan, Nepal, Bangladesh and many countries in Sub-Saharan Africa), may have the greatest barriers to female participation. In such situations, the only promising approach is the introduction of multiple components in the projects. By contrast in countries with low income but moderate social setting, expansion of places has itself been generally successful. However, even in these countries, establishing a link between the programs offered and the opportunities for women in the labor market was found to be critical. Expansion of places in non-traditional fields appears promising especially in countries (both low and middle income) with moderate social settings, but in the countries with difficult social settings, expansion of places in traditional fields may have to be the first step.

Introduction

The developmental payoffs to female primary and secondary schooling have been much researched and documented. The returns to both primary and secondary schooling--both economic and social--have been shown to be considerable across a wide spectrum of countries. Research has also shown that the returns to higher education are considerable, though not as high as for primary schooling (Psacharopoulos 1993).

The private economic returns include a shift in the allocation of women's time from non-market to market activities, e.g. wage employment and the market labor force, resulting in potential wage gains over their lifetimes. In addition, the economic externalities from higher education include the contribution to the GNP, increase in the tax base, and enhancement of the quality of the country's future leadership.

Social returns from women's higher education encompass not only fertility, child health, nutrition and schooling, but also an increase in productive opportunities, regional and occupational mobility, and upward income mobility of the household. The effects go beyond the women and their families, contributing to long run poverty alleviation.

Given the high returns to women's higher education, the economic case for promoting the access for all eligible women to higher education is strong. From the standpoint of gender equity, the case for unbiased selection from the pool of secondary school completers--men and women--is self-evident. Ensuring gender equity in higher education is important from an efficiency standpoint as well. Gender discrimination implies that a large number of potentially worthy candidates are denied the opportunity to be trained in specialized fields and contribute to the family's as well as the country's economic well-being.

Many aspects of higher education--quality, cost and efficiency, subsidization, and the like--have been investigated in considerable depth over the last couple of decades. However, few studies have examined the gender equity aspects of higher education. This paper makes a modest attempt to fill this gap.

An important feature of the higher education scenario over the last four decades is rapid expansion of places (and institutions) in developing countries.[2] The question that is of relevance from a gender perspective is how women fared in the wake of this expansion. This paper has five objectives:

a. Examine the trends in male and female enrollments, by region and by country, and note inter-regional differences, and intra-regional differences (section 2);

---

[2] In part this is due to very low initial levels at the time these countries became independent, and in part due to the political necessity to fulfill the rising aspirations of young people to obtain university education soon after the countries became independent. Whatever may have triggered this rapid expansion, it is widely believed (though not always proven with acceptable indicators) that it caused a decline in quality. The decline in quality is indisputable, but few studies have empirically disentangled the role of expansion from under-funding. For a recent analysis of these issues in the context of Sub Saharan Africa, see W. Saint (1992).

b. Separate out the change in the female enrollment ratio between two time periods into (i) expansion effect, (ii) gender disparity effect, and (iii) population composition effect, for every country for which data are available for at least ten most recent years (section 3);

c. Analyze the factors behind the observed changes in female enrollment rates and gender parity in enrollments, over the period 1970-1988, (section 4);

d. Examine the issue of gender streaming (section 5); and

e. Examine World Bank project experience, especially the trends in lending, the identified constraints, the interventions proposed in the projects and the lessons learned (Part II, Sections 6-11).

The overall conclusions and operational implications are summarized in the final section.

PART I - PROGRESS IN WOMEN'S HIGHER EDUCATION

1. Definitions and Data Base

1.1   Tertiary enrollment ratios show the number of men and women enrolled in tertiary institutions as a percentage of the respective populations of school age men and women. Unlike primary and secondary education, which correspond to a given number of grades, tertiary education encompasses many types of programs; the duration of study also differs between the programs. The definitions used here correspond to the International Standard Classification of Education (ISCED) which identifies three major types of programs, Levels 5, 6 and 7. Level 5 programs are practical in nature and prepare students for particular vocational fields, e.g., high level technicians, teachers and nurses. Level 6 refers to programs leading to a first university degree, and Level 7 represents post-graduate university degrees (UNESCO Statistical Yearbook, 1992). Our definition of tertiary enrollment is the sum of levels 5, 6 and 7. For analysis of gender streaming, e.g., enrollments by levels and fields, we have excluded Level 7 as they make up a very small percentage of the total. The data used here are UNESCO data drawn from the Bank Economic and Social Database (BESD). Data on the share of manufacturing and services in GDP are drawn from World Development Report (1991), and GDP per capita from Summers and Heston (1991). Data on the share of female labor supply in the service and manufacturing sectors is from the United Nations "Women's Indicators and Statistics Spreadsheet Database for Microcomputer" (WISTAT).

2. Overall Trends in Tertiary Enrollments, 1970-1988

2.1   In 1970, tertiary enrollments for men were low and those for women even lower in every region (see Figure 1). For example, in Sub-Saharan Africa only 0.91 percent of males and 0.14 percent of females aged 20-24 were enrolled in tertiary education. The enrollment rates were highest in Latin America region: the gross enrollment ratios were 9 percent for males and 5 percent for females. By 1988, enrollment rates for men had sharply increased in East Asia, Latin America and the Caribbean, the Middle East and North Africa. Enrollment rates for women lagged behind considerably, except in Latin America region where the "gender gap" (the difference between male and female enrollment) was virtually closed. In Sub-Saharan Africa men's enrollment tripled while women's enrollment grew seven-fold, thus narrowing the gender gap. Yet, the enrollment rates of both men and women were very low, compared to the rest of the world. Enrollments in South Asia showed the least improvement in terms of rate of change over the period 1970-88. However, the rates (of both men and women) in 1988 were higher than in Sub-Saharan Africa, though lower than the rest of the world.

2.2   These regional aggregates conceal substantial intra-regional differences in the average enrollment ratios for both men and women. For example, inter-country differences in LAC and West Africa regions with a relatively high average enrollment (see Figures 2 and 3) are about the same as in North Africa region with a relatively low average enrollment (see Figure 4).[3]

2.3   In order to analyze country performance by changes in gross enrollment rates **and** changes in gender ratio of enrollments, transition matrices were generated. For this purpose, **the** countries were grouped according to their level of average enrollment rates, as follows:

- those with a high enrollment rate (greater than 15 per cent);
- those with a mid-high rate (11 to 15 per cent);
- those with a mid-low rate (6 to 10 per cent); and
- those with a low rate (below 5 per cent).

Similar grouping was done according to the degree of gender parity (defined as the number of females per hundred males), as follows:

- those with a high gender parity (greater than 75 per cent);
- those with medium parity (45 to 75 per cent); and
- those with low parity (below 45 per cent).

---

[3] East Africa, East and South Asia graphs appear in the Appendix. Data for all figures is found in Appendix Table 1.

Figure 1: Tertiary Enrollments by Region, 1970 and 1988

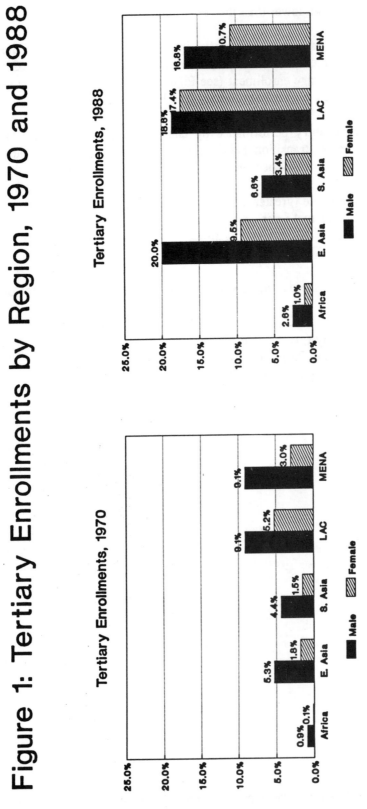

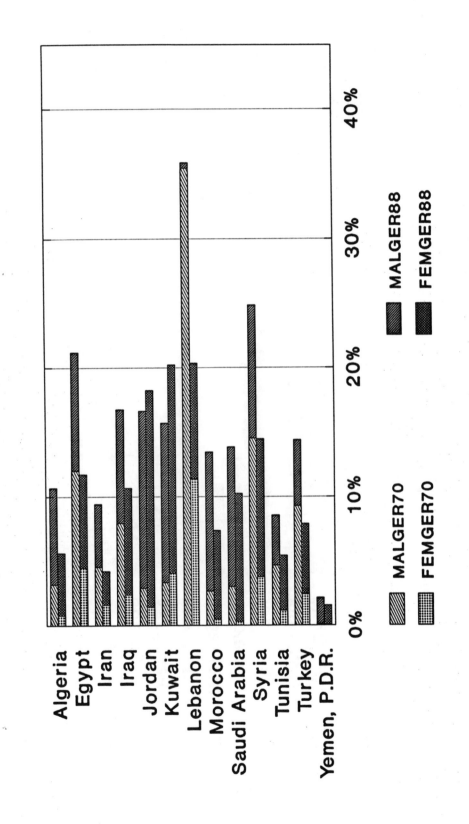

Figure 2: Tertiary Enrollments
North Africa/Middle East, 1970 and 1988

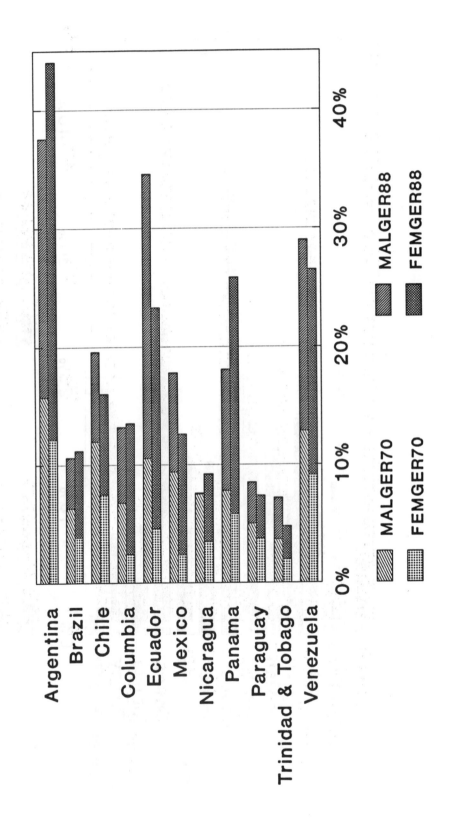

Figure 3: Tertiary Enrollments
Latin America & the Caribbean, 1970/1988

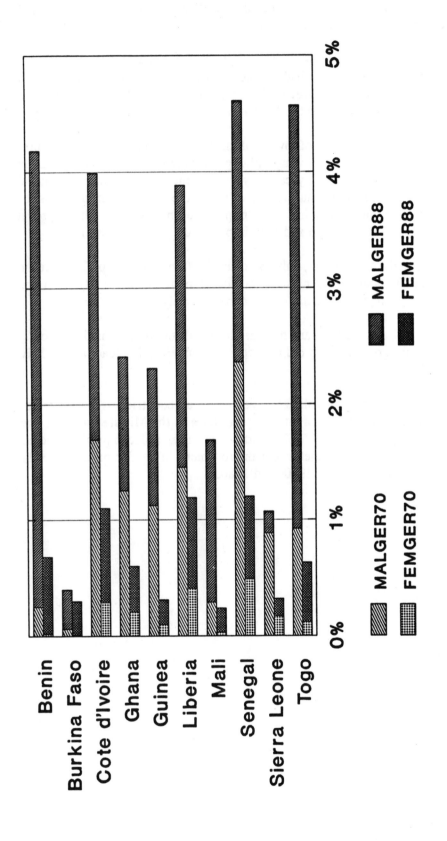

Figure 4: Tertiary Enrollments
Western Africa, 1970 and 1988

We recognize that any cut off points for such classifications are arbitrary. The purpose of this exercise is merely to illustrate the differences between countries with regard to the nature of their achievements.

2.4   The results are shown in Table 1. In Sub-Saharan Africa in 1970, all countries had very low enrollments and the majority had low gender parity. By 1988, average enrollment rates were still low for all countries; however, three shifted from low to medium gender parity. Botswana transitioned from low to high parity, and Lesotho from medium to high parity.

2.5   Similar situation of low enrollment rates and low gender parity prevailed in South Asian countries, with only Sri Lanka showing a high gender parity. By 1988 only Bangladesh remained in the low enrollment, low gender parity category. India increased enrollments and also improved gender parity. Pakistan represents the unusual case of very little change in enrollments, but an improvement in parity. In East Asia, only China had medium parity even in 1970; parity improved in all countries by 1988. Indonesia and Korea improved both in parity and in enrollment rates.

2.6   In the Middle East, only two countries (Syria and Egypt) had enrollment rates greater than 5 per cent in 1970, though gender parity was low in both countries. By 1988 only Kuwait and Jordan progressed towards high enrollments with improved parity.

2.7   In Latin America and the Caribbean, all countries transitioned to higher enrollments with parity by 1988. Progress in parity did not occur in Honduras, Trinidad, and El Salvador despite increase in average enrollment rates.

2.8   In summary, enrollments went up in all countries over the period 1970-88. However, **only in East Asia, Latin America and two countries in the Middle East can one discern progress in enrollments with gender parity.** The next section uses a decomposition methodology to assess the relative roles of average enrollments and improvement in gender parity in explaining the changes in female enrollment rates over the 1970s and 1980s.

Table 1: Transition Matrix for Changes in Tertiary Enrollment and Gender Parity, 1970-1988

Gender Ratio (Females per 100 males)	Total Average Enrollment Rates, 1970					Total Average Enrollment Rates, 1988			
	(LOW) 0-5%	(MID-LOW) 6-10%	(MID-HIGH) 11-15%	(HIGH) >15%		(LOW) 0-5%	(MID-LOW) 6-10%	(MID-HIGH) 11-15%	(HIGH) >15%
(HIGH) >75	Kuwait Sri Lanka		Argentina	Uruguay*		Botswana Lesotho	Brazil Nicaragua Paraguay	Columbia	Argentina Chile Jordan Kuwait Panama Uruguay Venezuela
(MED) 45-75	Brazil China* Honduras* Jordan Lesotho Madagascar Mozambique Nicaragua Paraguay Swaziland Trinidad/Tobago	Chile El Salvador* Panama	Venezuela			Burkina Faso China Lao, PDR Madagascar Mauritius Pakistan Sri Lanka Sudan' Swaziland Yemen, PDR	Algeria Honduras India' Indonesia' Iran Morocco Trinidad/Tobago Tunisia	Iraq Saudi Arabia Turkey	Ecuador Egypt El Salvador Korea, Rep. Mexico Syria
(LOW) <45	Algeria Bangladesh Benin Botswana* Burkina Faso Burundi Central African Republic* Chad Columbia Congo Cote D'Ivoire Ethiopia Gabon Ghana Guinea India Indonesia Iran Iraq Lao, PDR Liberia Malawi Mali Mauritania* Mauritius Mexico Morocco Nepal* Niger Nigeria Pakistan Rwanda Saudi Arabia Senegal Sudan Tanzania Togo Tunisia Turkey Uganda Yemen, PDR Zambia	Ecuador Egypt Korea, Rep. Syria				Bangladesh Benin Burundi Central African Republic Chad' Congo Cote D'Ivoire' Ethiopia Gabon Ghana Guinea Liberia Malawi Mali' Mauritania Mozambique Niger Nigeria Rwanda Senegal Tanzania Togo Uganda Zambia	Nepal		

Notes: * 1975 figures used for 1970, where 1970 data was not available.
       ' 1985 figures used for 1988, where 1988 data was not available.

3. Determinants of Female Enrollments

3.1   To a greater extent than in primary and secondary enrollments, women's (as well as men's) participation in higher education is influenced by socio-political factors (e.g. greater political pressures for opening more colleges/universities), economic factors including the prevailing private rates of return for higher education, the structural changes occurring in the economies, and deliberate, policy-induced changes in the gender ratio of enrollments. Figure 5 outlines the analytical framework used in this paper. In this section, a simple three-factor decomposition analysis of the factors underlying the changes in female enrollments is outlined and empirically verified. In the next section, an analysis of causality is attempted.

3.2   The Model. Suppose e_t is the total enrollment ratio (both males and females); f_t and m_t are female and male enrollments, respectively, then we have

$$e_t = a_t f_t + (1-a_t)m_t \tag{1}$$

where a_t is the proportion of females in the enrollment age groups. Suppose further that r_t is the ratio of females to males enrolled in the schools, then we must have

$$r_t = \frac{a_t f_t}{(1-a_t) m_t} \tag{2}$$

then (1) can be written as

$$f_t = \frac{r_t e_t}{a_t(1+r_t)} \tag{3}$$

Our objective is to explain this change in the female enrollment ratio $(f_t - f_{t-1})$ in terms of changes in e_t, r_t and a_t.

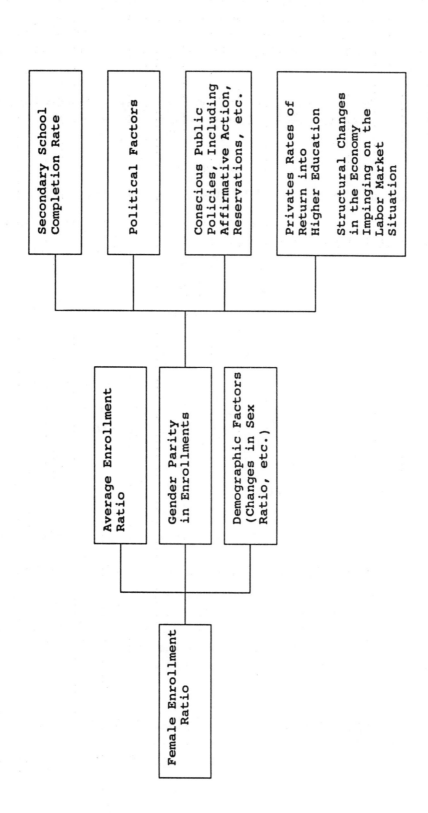

Figure 5: Determinants of Female Enrollments in Higher Education

The change due to e_t will be called expansion effect which is defined as

$$E_t = \left[\frac{f_{t-1}}{e_{t-1}} + \frac{f_t}{e_t} \right] \frac{(e_t - e_{t-1})}{f_{t-1}} * 100 \qquad (4)$$

Similarly, the change due to r_t will be called female-male enrollment disparity effect and is defined as

$$D_t = \left[\frac{f_{t-1}}{r_{t-1}(1+r_t)} + \frac{f_t}{r_t(1+r_{t-1})} \right] \frac{(r_t - r_{t-1})}{f_{t-1}} * 100 \qquad (5)$$

and finally the effect due to change in a_t will be called female-male population ratio effect and is defined as

$$A_t = - \left[\frac{f_{t-1}}{a_t} + \frac{f_t}{a_{t-1}} \right] \frac{(a_t - a_{t-1})}{f_{t-1}} * 100 \qquad (6)$$

And the total change in female enrollment ratio is given by

$$F_t = f_t - f_{t-1} = \frac{r_t e_t}{a_t (1+r_t)} - \frac{r_{t-1} e_{t-1}}{a_{t-1} (1+r_{t-1})} \qquad (7)$$

It can be seen from (4), (5), (6) and (7) that

$$F_t = E_t + D_t + A_t \qquad (8)$$

which shows that the total change in the female enrollment ratio is equal to the sum of changes due to three factors, namely, e_t, r_t and a_t.

3.3   The results from the above model for the determinants of average annual change in female tertiary enrollments over the period 1970-90 for 41 countries are summarized in Table 2.[4] The group

---

[4]The sample size is driven by the availability of time series data on enrollments for at least a ten-year period during 1970-1990. Results for individual countries are given in Appendix Table 2.

averages are given according to region, income and initial level of female enrollments. The results show that expansion of <u>average</u> enrollment was the <u>dominant</u> factor contributing to an improvement (positive change) in female enrollment ratio, accounting for about 70% of its change over the 1970s and 1980s. Expansion effect dominates no matter how the countries are classified. Quite clearly, women benefitted substantially from the general expansion of places in higher education.

3.4   What were the factors that contributed to the general expansion of higher education enrollments? Though this aspect is beyond the scope of this paper, a backdrop is necessary to appreciate the context since women benefitted from such expansion. In a recent excellent overview of the crisis in higher education in Sub-Saharan Africa, Saint (1992) notes that enrollments expanded faster than the capacity of the universities, and that the quality declined as a result of increased enrollments and reduced funding. According to Saint, "Burgeoning population, rapidly rising numbers of secondary graduates and persistent economic stagnation combine to make managing the social demand for access to higher education the single most difficult task faced by the tertiary sector in Sub-Saharan Africa today." (p.105) Saint sees the political pressures as a critical factor behind the expansion.

3.5   Saint's analysis of socio-political factors behind the expansion, and the diagnostics of the crisis, are highly persuasive. Yet, it is important to bear in mind the **economic** factors behind expansion as well. Available data on the private economic rates of return to higher education (see Figure 6) suggest that the private rate of return is the highest in Sub-Saharan Africa.[5] The high private rate of return for Sub-Saharan Africa is explainable by Saint's own analysis, who also notes that "In spite of the notable if uneven expansion of higher education enrollments over the past decade, access to the university remains relatively constrained." (p.27) Given the "tiny minority" of higher educated manpower (relative to the demand), private rates of return rule high, intensifying the political pressures for expansion.

3.6   The prevalence of high economic rates of return -- even from higher education of dubious quality -- coupled with expansion of higher education places, presumably helped women proportionately more than men, to the extent parents did see benefits from sending their daughters to the universities whose numbers have grown. Ideally, expansion, with due regard to quality, should have been the policy perspective. This did not happen. Saint rightly points out the resulting quantity-quality trade off; yet women improved their relative share with expansion.

3.7   Changes in gender parity of enrollments--whether driven by conscious public policies, or changes in labor market conditions induced by structural changes in the economies--also contributed to an increase in female enrollment albeit to a small extent, i.e., about 20-30 percent of the change in female enrollment ratio. The small contribution of changes in gender ratio is not surprising, to the extent gender parity itself changed only slowly in most countries. Its contribution is highest in the middle-low income countries.

3.8   Only in South Asia and Middle Eastern regions, demographic changes, i.e., the proportion of females to total population, seem to affect women's enrollment negatively. This is explainable by the pervasive sex bias against women in some countries resulting in a secular decline in the sex ratio (see Sen, 1989). The issue of adverse demographic (sex) ratios is not pursued in this paper.

---

[5]Interestingly, the variation across regions in the social rates of return is much lower.

Table 2: Average Annual Change in Female Tertiary Enrollment (1970s and 1980s)
Decomposed into Percent Change due to Expansion of Total Tertiary Enrollment and Disparity

N=41*	Number	Average Annual Change in Female Tertiary Enrollment	Expansion	Percent Due to Disparity	Population Change
REGIONS					
Africa	(15)	13.5	70.6	29.3	0.2
South Asia	(4)	8.2	71.0	29.5	-0.5
East Asia	(6)	10.7	78.3	20.5	1.3
MENA	(10)	13.1	72.0	30.1	-2.0
LAC	(6)	14.6	70.9	28.6	0.4
INCOME					
Low	(18)	12.8	73.8	26.3	-0.1
Middle-Low	(12)	12.8	64.6	34.4	1.0
Middle-High	(6)	9.1	77.1	22.1	0.8
High	(5)	15.9	78.4	26.7	-5.1
INITIAL LEVEL OF FEMALE TERTIARY ENROLLMENTS					
Low (<1)	(21)	13.7	72.1	27.9	0.0
Medium (1-4)	(11)	10.6	71.7	28.4	-0.1
High (>4)	(9)	12.6	72.7	28.2	-1.0

* Sample Represents: 69.4% of LDC population
                        33.8% of Sub-Saharan Africa
                        86.4% of South Asia

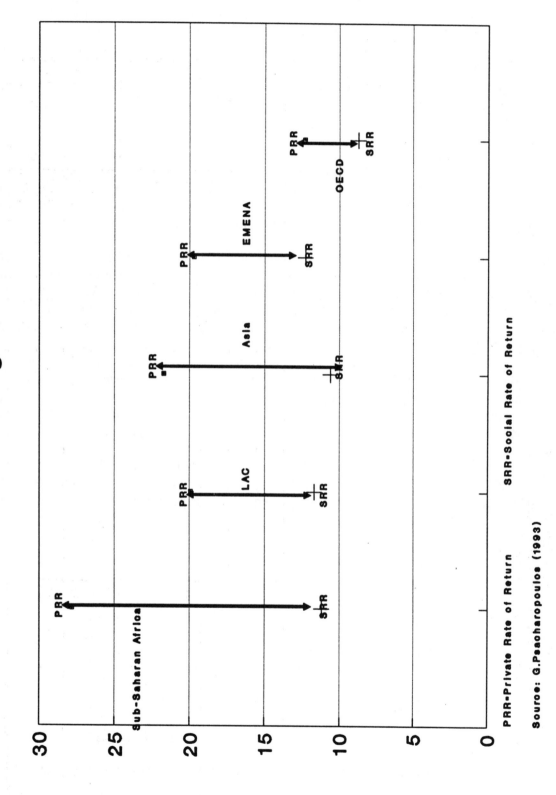

Figure 6: Private & Social Rates of Return to Higher Education

PRR=Private Rate of Return

SRR=Social Rate of Return

Source: G.Psacharopoulos (1993)

4. Alternative Explanations for Low Female Enrollments

4.1   Of the many socio-economic/cultural factors inhibiting women's participation in higher education, three are worth noting. First, low secondary school enrollments greatly reduce the scope for progress in higher education. Second, even if secondary enrollments were high, the dropout rates of girls in some countries are so high as to result in only a small pool of completers eligible for higher education. Third, from the demand side, the low level of manufacturing and service activities may discourage parents from sending their girls for university education as they do not see prospects for absorption in the formal labor market. The relative strength of each of these factors may vary across the countries.

4.2   To know the extent to which low secondary enrollment constrained higher education participation rates of women, we related female tertiary enrollments to lagged secondary enrollment. Figure 7 shows that female tertiary enrollment is generally high in countries where the secondary enrollment rates (appropriately lagged) are also high. This simple, highly aggregative relationship, however, does not take into account the problem of high dropout rates among girls.

4.3   Wastage--dropout and repetition--is high in most developing countries: the proportion of students completing primary school in low-income countries is less than two-thirds and has fallen further in recent years. Data on dropout and repetition rates are scarce. Where available, they do indicate a higher proportion for girls than for boys. In Bangladesh, only 5 percent of pupils entering grade 1 complete grade 12; the dropout rate for girls is higher than for boys at all levels. Available country-specific evidence shows that this is true across regions (see Herz et al., 1991). A good indicator of student flow rates is the proportion of secondary school completers by gender, which enables comparisons of secondary school completion rates with higher education enrollment rates, by gender. Unfortunately, such a cohort analysis is impossible, given the low country coverage and poor quality of available data.[6] The problems of the low enrollments at the secondary school and low survival rates have to be addressed in order to improve women's chances of entry into higher education.

4.4   The third factor is: to what extent female enrollments in higher education are affected by the structure of the economy as reflected in the size of the modern manufacturing sector and services sector.[7] Figure 8 shows that the gender parity in enrollment is positively correlated with the size of the service and manufacturing sectors.

---

[6]See Fredriksen, 1991, for a thorough overview of the issue and alternative methodologies.

[7]We examined the correlation between female enrollment rate, and gender parity in total enrollments, with a GDP per capita, and found it to be rather weak.

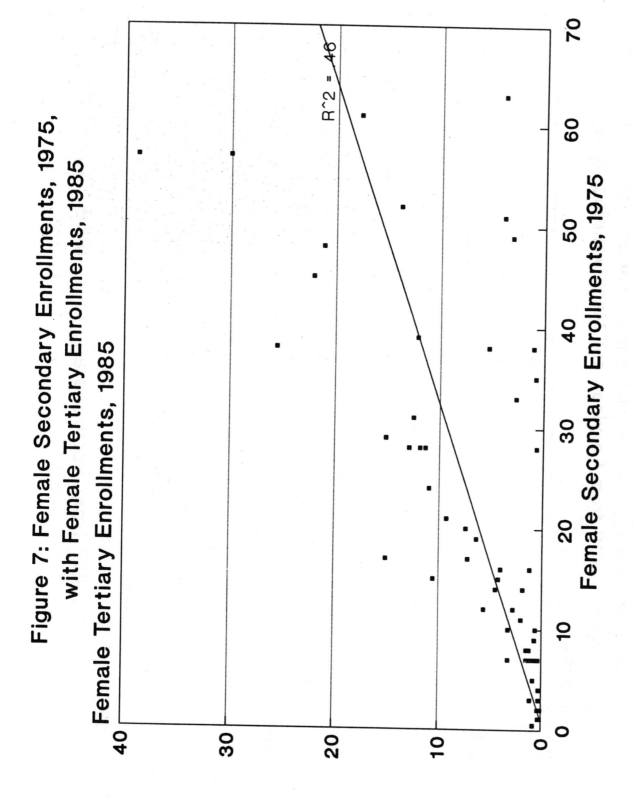

Figure 7: Female Secondary Enrollments, 1975, with Female Tertiary Enrollments, 1985

Figure 8: Females per 100 Males in Higher Education, 1985
with % GDP from Services and Manufacturing, 1988

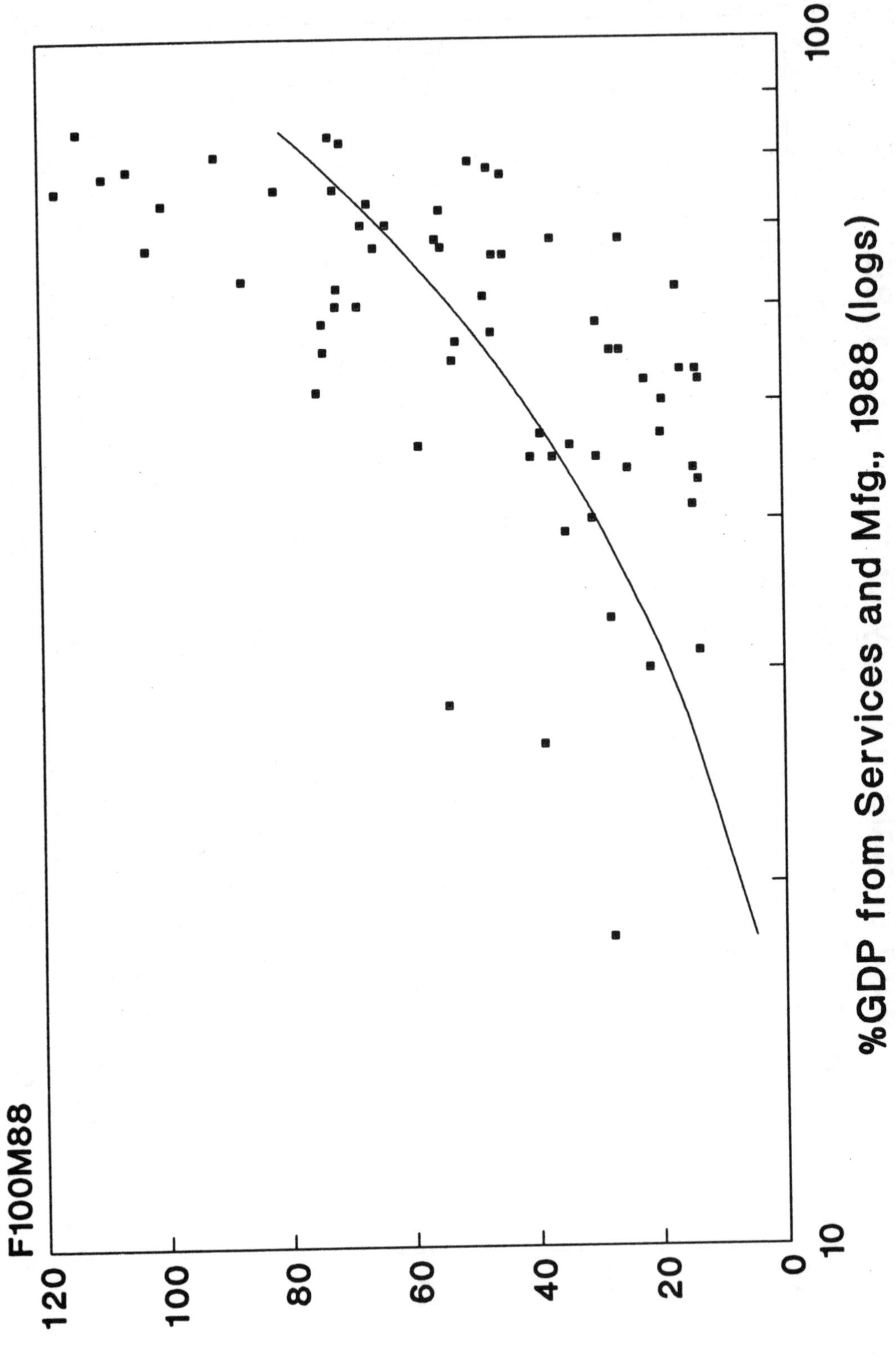

4.5 <u>Determinants of gender parity</u>. We have attempted a quantitative analysis of the determinants of gender parity, utilizing the small sample of countries for which the data are available (n=41). We hypothesize that gender parity in enrollments in 1988 is determined by (a) the initial level of average enrollments ($LTOT_{70}$), (b) the growth rate of average enrollments (GRATE), and (c) the economic structure variables (FL80SER). Table 3 presents the results of log-linear regressions for alternative model specifications. The basic model is:

$$F100m88 = \alpha + \beta_1(LTOT_{70}) + \beta_2(GRATE) + \beta_3(FL80SER) + e \qquad (9)$$

where

> F100m88 = Females per 100 males enrolled in 1988
> $LTOT_{70}$ = Log Total Enrollments in 1970
> GRATE = Growth Rate of Average Enrollments 1970-88
> FL80SER = Proportion of females in the total labor force in the Services Sector.

To overcome potential endogeneity, the above equation was estimated with Two-Stage Least Squares (TSLS) estimation technique, instrumenting out FL80SER using FL70SER.

4.6 As is clear from Table 3, the initial level of enrollments and the growth rate of enrollments are highly significant consistently in all equations. Female employment in services is significant, when <u>not</u> controlled with a dummy for LAC region.[8] Clearly, the results lend support to the overwhelming role of supply of tertiary places in the observed (small) improvement in the gender ratio in higher education enrollments over the period 1970-88.

4.7 Since expansion benefitted women proportionately more than men, <u>contraction</u> of places following educational adjustment reforms <u>may</u> hurt women more than men. However, as yet no <u>direct</u> evidence of adverse effect of contraction of higher education enrollments on women is available. A recent study of the East African experience of rationing of higher education places suggests that such rationing resulted in higher education for the wealthy (Knight and Sabot, 1990); unfortunately the impact was not disaggregated by gender. While more needs to be learned about similar impacts of contraction of higher education by gender through micro studies, policy-makers in the countries implementing educational reforms need at least be cautioned about the <u>possible</u> adverse impact on women, so that appropriate safety nets are built to ensure gender equity in the wake of reform.

---

[8] We have also estimated an equation with log RGDP85 but the coefficient is not significant.

Table 3: Determinants of Gender Parity

Independent Variables	Dependent Variable: F100M88		
	Equation 1	Equation 2	Equation 3
α	24.83* (3.085)	33.36* (4.09)	-0.17 (-0.004)
$LTOT_{70}$	17.83* (6.56)	12.56* (4.29)	16.38* (4.626)
GRATE	1.66* (2.04)	1.40* (2.14)	1.88* (2.572)
FL80SER	0.525* (2.06)	0.13ns (0.49)	--
LOG(RGDP85)	--	--	5.65 (1.008)
DUMLAC	--	25.5* (2.75)	--
R^2	0.53	0.59	0.49
n	49	49	49

Notes: Definitions of variables are given in the text. DUMLAC stands for dummy for Latin American Countries. Figures in brackets represent t-values.

* Coefficient statistically significant at 5% level or more.

ns Coefficient statistically not significant.

5.   Gender Streaming

5.1   The growth in female tertiary enrollments since 1970 conceals the fact that women are over-represented in the vocational schools and commercial/secretarial training schools (UNESCO, 1985). Figure 9 shows the female/male ratio in technical/vocational enrollments and university enrollments across regions for two time periods. In Sub-Saharan Africa, Latin America and the Caribbean, and the Middle East and North Africa, women are better represented in the technical and vocational schools in 1970. By 1980-84 the gap in the female/male ratio between technical/vocational and university enrollments widened considerably in LAC. Sub-Saharan Africa and the Middle East/North Africa regions registered little progress, and South and East Asia remained the only regions where women were better represented in the university stream.

5.2   Figures 10 and 11 show the gender ratio by fields of study by regions, and by per capita income group, respectively. The fields are classified broadly into two groups: (1) Arts, encompassing education and social sciences, and (2) Sciences, including natural and medical sciences and agriculture. Across regions, the gender ratio is higher for arts than for the sciences. The differences are especially marked in East Asia and Latin America and the Caribbean for the period 1980-84. LAC region has the highest female/male ratio in tertiary enrollments; yet when this is decomposed by fields, the ratio for sciences is less than 25 per cent. The lowest gender parity in sciences is to be found in Sub-Saharan Africa and South Asia, which also have lowest parity overall. Interestingly, the OECD countries have high overall parity, but parity in sciences in 1980-84 is less than in the LAC and MENA regions. To this extent, "gender streaming" is a problem pervasive in both developing and developed countries.

5.3   In Figure 11, the gender ratio data for different countries are averaged according to per capita income levels. Not surprisingly, the gender ratios for both sciences and arts improve with income level, with the exception of the very high income group for 1980-84.

5.4   The above analysis suggests that even though enrollments and gender parity may improve further in many countries, gender streaming is likely to persist; it is unlikely to disappear with development. Therefore, conscious public policies, including incentives such as scholarships, are required at the secondary school level (to induce girls to opt for mathematics and sciences) and at the university level.

5.5   The paucity of gender-disaggregated data on enrollments is a major concern in analyzing women in higher education. As the data in Appendix Table 1 show, serious gaps exist in the time series data on enrollment rates by gender in all regions. The small sample size in our analysis of the average annual change in female tertiary enrollments is a reflection of the fact that ten years of consecutive, gender-disaggregated data on tertiary enrollments was available for less than a third of the countries in Latin America and the Caribbean, less than half of the countries in Sub-Saharan Africa, and a little more than half of the countries in Asia and the Middle East/North Africa.

5.6   Our analysis of the determinants of female enrollments was severely constrained not only by the lack of consecutive time series data on enrollments from 1970-90 but also the low country coverage and poor quality of available data on either dropout rates at the secondary level or the proportion of secondary school completers disaggregated by gender. Therefore, causality could not be established on what determines the level of female tertiary enrollments. However, simple correlations do suggest that lagged female secondary enrollments are positively correlated to female tertiary enrollments.

5.7   The trends in the Bank's lending to higher education, the constraints identified, and the effectiveness of policies and programs formulated in the projects for enhancing female enrollments and improving representation in sciences are examined with reference to World Bank project experience in Part II.

Figure 9: Females per 100 Males by Level, 1970–74 and 1980–84

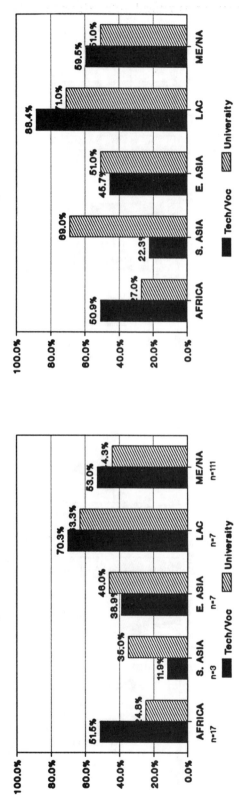

Females per 100 Males in Tertiary Educ. for the period 1975–79

Females per 100 Males in Tertiary Educ. for the period 1980–84

Figure 10: Females per 100 Males by Regions and Field of Study, 1970–74 and 1980–84

Females per 100 Males in Tertiary Educ.
by Field, 1970–74 (5 yr. av.)

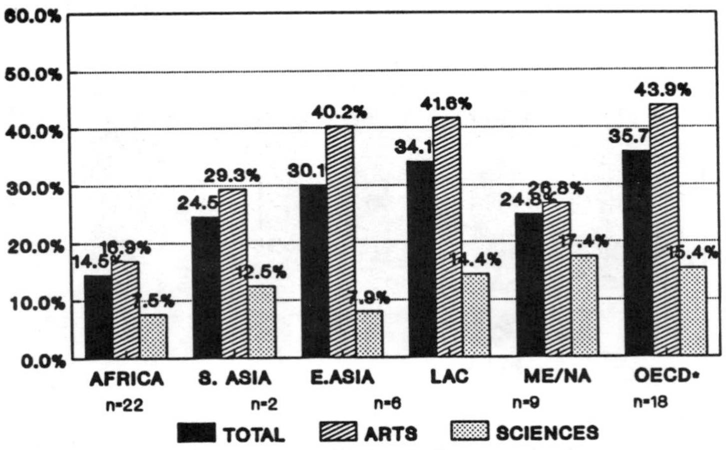

Females per 100 Males in Tertiary Educ.
by Field, 1980–84 (5 yr. av.)

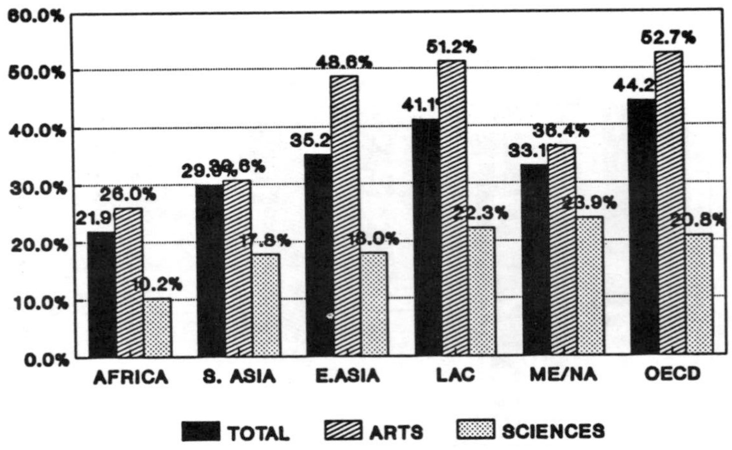

* OECD minus the US and Yugoslavia due to missing data.

Figure 11: Females per 100 Males by Income Group and Field of Study, 1970-74 and 1980-84

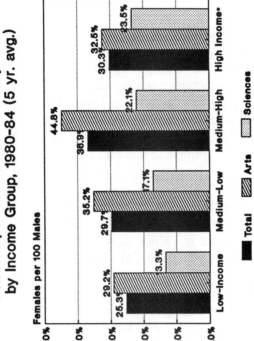

Females per 100 Males in Tertiary Educ.
by Income Group, 1970-74 (5 yr. avg.)

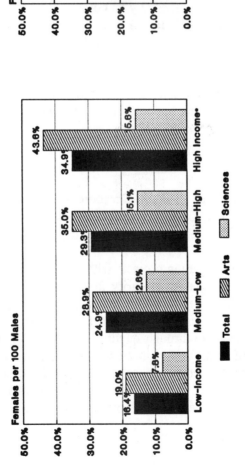

Females per 100 Males in Tertiary Educ.
by Income Group, 1980-84 (5 yr. avg.)

*OECD countries with Hong Kong, Singapore, Saudi Arabia & Singapore.

PART II - WORLD BANK PROJECT EXPERIENCE IN HIGHER EDUCATION

6. Overview

6.1   The World Bank began lending for education in 1963. The shift in Bank[9] investment precipitated from changes in economic thought in the early 1960s when education came to be seen as a critical investment in human capital essential to the development process. The objectives of many early education projects were to build infrastructures such as schools and to develop educational planning capacity. Since the early 1980s, the Bank-assisted projects have introduced policy reforms affecting the expansion, financing and internal efficiency especially of higher education systems. The reforms were designed to reduce uncontrolled growth of higher education expenditures by capping university intake, limiting grants and subsidies to students, introducing student fees, and rationalizing academic programs and staffing (Eisemon, 1992).

6.2   Despite the persistence of gender disparity in higher education in most developing countries, Bank-assisted projects between 1970-1985 rarely mentioned gender disparity as an issue or introduced significant policies to overcome it. More significantly, there was no coherent Bank policy regarding women's access to education in general and to higher education in particular.

6.3   Since the mid-1980s, however, Bank-assisted projects have increasingly paid attention to gender issues in higher education, notwithstanding the lack of a coherent policy regarding women's access to higher education. The analysis focuses especially on policies and project components which have been effective in increasing women's opportunities in higher education and draws lessons for the future. Section 7 reviews the methodology and data sources used for the study. Section 8 examines trends the Bank's lending to higher education projects by regions and over time (1972-1981 and 1982-1992) from a gender perspective. In Section 9, we analyze the constraints, and Section 10 provides an analysis of projects with specific interventions to increase female enrollment. In Section 11, promising approaches and lessons learned are examined with the hope of improving women's access to higher education for future higher education projects.

7. Methodology and Data

7.1   In this section, we cover all Bank education projects with higher education components from 1972-1992, including formal and non-formal programs leading to a degree, certificate or diploma. It also covers teacher training projects for which secondary degrees are pre-requisites for admittance.

7.2   In examining Bank education projects with higher education components, we classified them according to their sensitivity to gender disparity in enrollment rates at the tertiary level and the degree to which the projects introduce specific policy interventions to improve women's access to higher education. Thus, there are two main categories. The first category includes projects which at the minimum recognized gender as an issue through qualitative analysis of women's participation in post-secondary education and/or identified the constraints associated with low levels of enrollment. These are considered as projects which "acknowledge gender". The second includes projects which go beyond merely recognizing gender as an issue and introduce specific interventions to increase female participation and/or access to higher education. The central focus of the section is on this second category of projects

---

[9] The word "Bank" used in this section refers to the World Bank.

that contained specific policy interventions aimed at promoting greater gender parity. These projects are analyzed separately and in depth.

7.3   Primary resources for this study were World Bank Staff Appraisal Reports (SARs) for higher education projects between 1972 and 1992. For the purpose of analysis, we focused on education projects for which higher education comprised 25% or more of the total project cost. These also included education sector projects and teacher training projects.

7.4   For assessing possible shifts in the Bank's approach to gender equity in higher education over time, we analyzed two time periods: 1972-1981 and 1982-1992. The expectation is that the Bank may have paid greater attention to gender equity in projects in the more recent period.

7.5   Further material was extracted from Project Completion Reports (PCRs) and the Project Performance Audit Reports (PARs) and served as an evaluative tool for assessing project success in attaining the gender objectives stated in the SARs. To analyze the preliminary results of recent on-going projects with gender specific interventions, we interviewed project staff for selected countries.

7.6   Limitations of the Study. Notwithstanding the comprehensive coverage, the study has certain limitations in the selection and evaluation of projects. First, the study is limited only to the Bank's experience from 253 education projects with higher education components between 1972-1992. As such, it does not capture non-Bank project experience.

7.7   Second, limited gender awareness does not necessarily indicate a significant gender parity problem. For instance, in the Philippines, near parity in higher education enrollment exists. Not surprisingly, projects in the Philippines do not refer to the existence of a gender problem.[10] On the other hand, in the Gambia, where gender disparity at the tertiary level is great, failure to recognize the inequity would indicate low gender-sensitivity in Bank-assisted higher education projects.

7.8   Analyzing individual projects without understanding the government's overall plan for post-secondary education is not entirely satisfactory. In countries where primary enrollment rates remain excessively low, policies may focus on increasing access to and expansion of basic education, with less regard to gender parity in higher education. With these caveats, let us examine the trends in Bank lending to higher education.

8.   Trends in the Bank's Lending to Higher Education

8.1   Bank Lending. Overall, the Bank approved 122 higher education projects between 1972-1981 and 131 projects between 1982-1992 in Sub-Saharan Africa, East and South Asia, MENA and Latin America and the Caribbean. Of the 122 projects identified between 1972-1981, 32 (or 26% of total projects) acknowledged gender as an issue and 13 (or 11% of the total projects) introduced significant interventions to overcome gender disparity. The number as well as the proportion of projects addressing gender significantly increased during 1982-1992. Fifty-three (or 41% of the total higher education projects) recognized gender as an issue while 36 (28%) introduced specific interventions.

---

[10] However, even in these countries, women may be opting for low-paying, traditional fields of study. This issue of gender streaming could not be effectively addressed in this section owing to insufficient data base.

8.2   Resources for Gender Specific Interventions. Ideally, to determine the most cost-effective approaches to increasing gender equity in higher education, one would have to examine the costs associated with each gender-specific intervention. This was not possible, given the paucity of disaggregated data from project SARs. We can, however, estimate the amount invested in projects with gender components as a part of total higher education investment. Examination of the total investment allocated to specific projects may illustrate the relative weight placed on projects addressing gender equity within the context of higher education projects. Table 4 below compares the distribution of total number and costs of Bank-assisted higher education projects by region for 1972-1981 and 1982-1992.

8.3   1972-1981. The total cost of higher education projects approved between 1972 and 1981 was US $4.2 billion.[11] Interestingly, only 24% ($1 billion) of the total investments in higher education funded projects which acknowledged gender as an issue. Further, only 41% of the funding for projects acknowledging gender as an issue was allocated to projects with gender- specific policies ($420 million or 10% of total higher education investments). These figures suggest that projects acknowledging gender disparity did not receive primary attention from the Bank during the 1970s.

8.4   1982-1992. During the 1980s however, the situation improved with respect to addressing gender issues in higher education projects. While the total investment in Bank-assisted higher education projects was $7.8 billion, investment in projects acknowledging gender as an issue constituted 46% of the total costs for all higher education projects. The investment in projects introducing gender specific policies was 36% of total higher education investment (up from 10% in the 1970s).

Regional Distribution

8.5   a) All higher education projects. The distribution of education projects with higher education components reveals significant regional shifts in Bank lending strategies over time. Between 1972-1981, Sub-Saharan Africa accounted for the largest regional share or 38% of 122 higher education projects. Despite an increase in the total number of higher education projects from 1972-1981 to 1982-1992, Sub-Saharan Africa's share decreased during the later period to 27%. Much of the increase in total projects in the 1980s can be attributed to an increase in the number of projects allocated to East Asia from 23 (1972-1981) to 41 (1982-1992) (see Figures 12a and 12b).

8.6   With regard to total investment in higher education projects for both decades, the percent invested was highly skewed in favor of East Asia (54% during the 1970s and 65% during the 1980s). It is interesting to note that while Sub-Saharan Africa had a higher number of projects between 1972-1981, East Asia had a higher share of investment (Sub-Saharan Africa, 9%; East Asia, 54%). This trend continued in the 1980s. Whereas both East Asia and Sub-Saharan Africa had large numbers of higher education projects between 1982-1992, only 5% of total investment in higher education during that period was in Sub-Saharan Africa while East Asia received 65%.

8.7   b) Projects acknowledging gender. The largest number of higher education projects acknowledging gender as an issue during the 1970s was in the MENA region (41%). Projects acknowledging gender in MENA were comparatively well funded, receiving 65% of higher education investment during that period. MENA was followed by Sub-Saharan Africa in both instances (see Figures 13a and 13b).

---

[11] All figures are expressed in 1985 dollars.

Table 4: Review of Bank-Assisted Higher Education Projects

	1972-1981						1982-1992*					
	Sub-Saharan Africa	South Asia	East Asia	MENA	LAC	Total	Sub-Saharan Africa	South Asia	East Asia	MENA	LAC	Total
1. All Education Projects	62	11	36	35	30	174	71	23	58	40	37	229
2. Education Projects with higher education components (including teacher training)												
(a) Number of projects	46	6	23	28	19	122	35	13	41	29	13	131
(b) Total investment (Millions of US$)**	363.4	194.9	2282.7	1300.4	65.8	4207.2	417.2	623.6	5102.2	1027.1	622.0	7792.1
3. Those acknowledging gender issues												
(a) Number of projects	9	3	4	13	3	32	9	8	20	10	6	53
(b) Total investment (Millions of US$)**	162.9	83.6	77.5	669.4	29.8	1023.4	198.6	530.9	2310.1	419.7	84.3	3543.6
4. Projects with significant action to address gender problem***												
(a) Number of projects	4	2	1	4	2	13	5	6	14	8	3	36
(b) Total investment (Millions of US$)**	113.2	71.8	7.8	205.2	21.8	419.9	112.3	520.3	1832.5	321.0	15.8	2800.9
5. (a) Row 3 as a % of row 2												
(i) Number of projects	19.6%	50.0%	17.4%	46.4%	15.8%	26.2%	25.7%	61.5%	48.7%	34.5%	46.2%	40.5%
(ii) Total investment (Millions of US$)**	44.9%	42.9%	3.4%	51.5%	45.3%	24.3%	47.6%	85.1%	45.3%	40.9%	13.6%	45.5%
(b) Row 4 as a % of row 2												
(i) Number of projects	8.7%	33.3%	4.3%	14.3%	10.5%	10.6%	14.3%	46.1%	34.1%	27.6%	23.1%	27.5%
(ii) Total investment (Millions of US$)**	31.2%	36.8%	0.3%	15.8%	3.1%	9.9%	26.9%	83.4%	35.9%	31.3%	2.5%	35.9%

Source: *cut-off date May 31, 1992; **Expressed in 1985 dollars; ***Inclusive of monitoring, needs assessment and other government interventions.

30

Figure 12a: Education Projects w/Higher Education 1972-1981

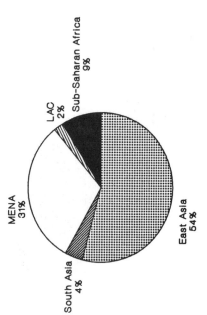

Total Investment in Higher Education 1972-1981

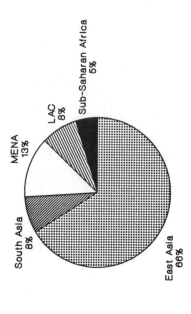

Figure 12b: Education Projects w/Higher Education 1982-1992

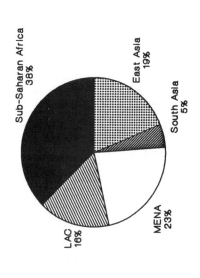

Total Investment in Higher Education 1982-1992

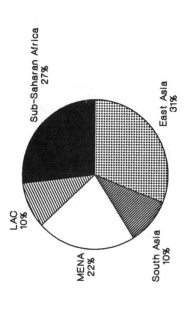

Source: Calculated from Table 4

Figure 13a: Ed Projects Acknowledging Gender 1972–1981

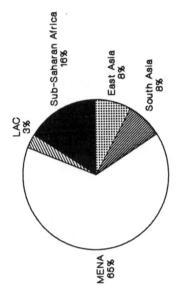

Total Investment in Ed. Projects Acknowledging Gender 1972–1981

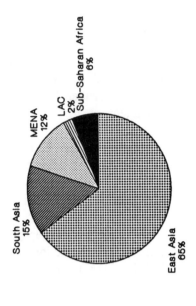

Figure 13b: Ed. Projects Acknowledging Gender 1982–1992

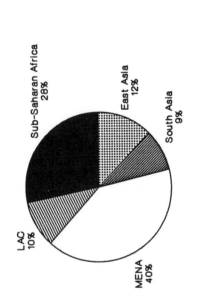

Total Investment in Ed. Projects Acknowledging Gender 1982–1992

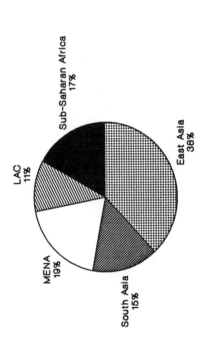

Source: Calculated from Table 4.

8.8   However, there was a substantial regional shift during the 1980s away from the MENA and Sub-Saharan Africa regions to the Asian regions in the numbers and investment in projects acknowledging gender. The number of projects in East Asia increased from 12% to 38%; the percent invested in these projects also grew from 8% to a surprising 65% (see Figures 14a and 14b). South Asia also experienced increases as the number of projects grew from 9% of the total projects to 15% and investment increased from 8% of the total investment to 15%. Looking at the Asian regions together for 1982-1992, a noticeable dominance appears in both the number of and investment in higher education projects acknowledging gender. The Asian regions together account for 53% of projects and 80% of the total project investment.

8.9   Total investment in higher education projects acknowledging gender in the Sub-Saharan African region during the 1980s decreased to a mere 6% from 16% in the 1970s. The LAC region only received 2% of the total amount invested in higher education projects acknowledging gender, but there was a higher degree of gender parity in the region.[12]

8.10   c) Projects with specific interventions. Regional distribution of the number of projects which introduced gender-specific interventions during 1972-1981 shows the highest number of projects in both the MENA (31%) and Sub-Saharan Africa (31%) regions (see Figures 14a and 14b). Additionally, relative to other areas, both MENA and Sub-Saharan Africa received the greatest portion of investment, MENA leading investment allocation with 49% and Sub-Saharan Africa following with 27%. Between 1982-1992, East Asia led in projects with specific interventions, with 39% of the projects with significant gender-specific actions, and 65% of total Bank investment on such projects in all regions.

8.11   To summarize, over the last two decades, the Bank's involvement in higher education has increased both in the number of projects and the volume of lending, despite a shift in overall Bank lending from higher education to primary and secondary education during the 1980s. Regional project distributions indicate that East Asia received the largest amount of lending for higher education over the past two decades and tried a wider variety of specific interventions to reduce gender disparity. Bank-assisted projects in all regions gave more emphasis in gender issues in higher education in the 1980s than in the 1970s.

---

[12] Although LAC enjoys relative parity in tertiary enrollment, there remain "streaming" issues that affect female employment.

33

Figure 14a: Projects with Interventions 1972–1981

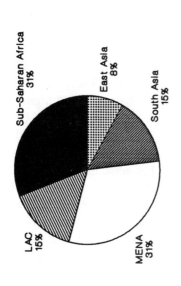

Investment in Intervention Projects 1972–1981

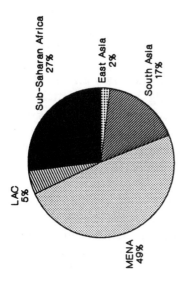

Figure 14b: Projects with Interventions 1982–1992

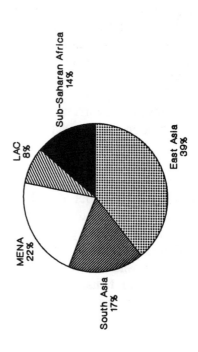

Investment in Intervention Projects 1982–1992

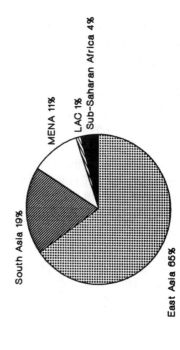

Source: Calculated from Table 4.

9.   Constraints to Female Participation

9.1   The specific interventions introduced need to be assessed against the backdrop of the specific constraints to women's participation in particular countries. The important questions are: What factors inhibit gender parity at the tertiary level? Which interventions (if any) have been introduced to overcome these identified constraints? Which are the successful interventions? Are there regional variations in constraints and interventions?

9.2   The constraints on female participation in higher education vary across regions and even within countries; however, certain patterns in constraints affecting women's participation in post-secondary education exist among most regions. One obvious initial constraint shared by several countries is the small pool of students completing secondary school. It is very difficult to increase women's access to higher education without raising female enrollments at the secondary level. Even if a pool of qualified female students exists at the secondary level, a number of other constraints inhibit women's participation in higher education.

9.3   Societal Constraints. Few projects identified the social constraints to women's enrollment. One such constraint is parental attitudes towards educating their daughters. Only four out of 49 projects which introduced gender-specific policies to increase women's access to higher education underlined the importance of social barriers on female participation in higher education.[13] Ignoring social barriers in projects often results in failing to achieve targeted goals for female participation. For example, a recent project in Nepal introduced expansion-related policies in order to raise the low level of female participation in tertiary education including reserving places for female students and providing dorm facilities. However, the preliminary results of the project indicate that the objectives for female participation set at the appraisal have not been achieved despite the project's interventions due to low private demand for education. Presently, a study is underway to examine the social constraints to female participation in higher education in Nepal.

9.4   Program of Study: Traditional vs. Non-Traditional Curriculum. The types of programs available to women in tertiary education also seem to affect female enrolment at the tertiary level. In some countries, the existence of an imperfect link between education and the labor market is cited as a major obstacle affecting women's participation in tertiary education. Often women are channelled into traditional fields of study irrespective of market conditions. Lack of marketability of women with post-secondary education can then act as a deterrent, discouraging women from seeking higher education.

9.5   Unequal Access to Quality Secondary Education. Unequal access to secondary education and poor quality of secondary education received by girls in much of Sub-Saharan Africa and East Asia has resulted in a limited pool of qualified female candidates for higher education (see Lee and Lockheed 1989). Unfortunately, the disadvantage women have in university entrance exams, due to lower quality of secondary education and girls' lower access rates to secondary education, often goes unnoticed and has been addressed in only a few projects. But a project in Tunisia identified the low representation of women in science and math related disciplines at the secondary education level as a main factor of the low participation of female students in science and technology-related fields at the tertiary level. Moreover, girls' tendency to have lower completion rates at the primary and secondary levels was noted

---

[13] By contrast, the negative attitudes of parents towards their daughters education at the primary and secondary education levels have received relatively better attention in projects.

as a major obstacle to women's access to higher education in projects in China, Malawi, Mali, and Niger.

9.6   <u>Lack of Dorm Facilities</u>. In general, higher education institutions in most developing countries are established in relatively well developed urban areas. Most people, especially from rural areas, have limited access to higher education because of the distance to higher education institutions. The distance problem is a particularly critical obstacle for women since parents often are concerned about their daughters' transportation to distant institutions and about their living alone. Provision of culturally appropriate boarding facilities is often used as an approach to reduce the distance problem to increase female participation in tertiary education, and lack of boarding facilities is identified as a barrier to female participation. However, only three projects identified the lack of culturally appropriate boarding facilities as a constraint on female participation in tertiary education.

10.   Interventions

10.1   One interesting trend observable across all regions throughout both decades is the tendency to introduce gender-specific interventions without proper analysis of the gender barriers (see Appendix Table 3). For instance, when enrollment rates for women are relatively low, often it is believed that simple expansion of school places and/or provision of boarding facilities for female students will increase the enrollments of women in higher education. The results of such an assumption have often been disappointing because the low participation rate of women in higher education may be due to factors other than lack of space or accommodation. Failure to recognize these factors may prohibit the project from realizing the objectives set at appraisal (see Box 1).

Box 1: Projects Without a Critical Analysis of Constraints

In some countries simple expansion of student places may not result in an increase woman's access if household demand for higher education is weak. In such a case, identifying constraints on female education and introducing specific policies to overcome them are key to having a successful project.

In response to the observed shortage of female teachers (i.e. favorable demand situation in the labor market), Pakistan's Third Education Project (1977) attempted to increase output of female teachers by construction and expansion of female teacher training institutes. Female teacher training capacity was increased by 50%. But the PAR (1990) found that although the expansion objective was ultimately achieved, project facilities had been consistently under-utilized and under-enrolled.

Morocco's Fourth Education Project also sought to increase the output of both male and female skilled teachers by expanding five different post-secondary education institutions. All programs would be open to women, with a target 20% female enrollment. The PCR found that the five higher education institutions assisted under the project remain under-enrolled. Only one third of the target enrollment figures was achieved.

Similarly, Morocco's Fifth Education Project assisted with the construction and equipping of four secondary teacher training institutes in science and mathematics, with 3,860 student places (of which about-one third would be for women). However, the PCR found that enrollments are well below the specific objectives set at the appraisal.

A recent Bank-assisted project in Nepal provided dorm facilities and reserved student spaces for girls. However, the preliminary results of the project indicate that the objectives of the project set at the appraisal have not been achieved due to low private demand for education.

These examples of underutilization of the existing capacity suggests that mere expansion of places is not enough when multiple social and/or economic barriers inhibit female participation in higher education. Further research and analysis of the constraints is necessary to formulate appropriate strategies to overcome them.

10.2   The identification of constraints on female participation in higher education varies considerably across regions. Within the MENA and Sub-Saharan Africa regions, most interventions were introduced without regard to gender constraints affecting women's access to higher education. This mismatch between identified constraints and interventions is the primary reason for the observed low enrollment at the tertiary level notwithstanding expansion of higher education institutions.

10.3   In comparison with the MENA and Sub-Saharan Africa regions, projects in South Asia and East Asia analyzed constraints inhibiting female participation in higher education more closely. In Latin America and the Caribbean, projects fail either to identify the barriers affecting women's access to higher education or to propose interventions to overcome them. Yet LAC countries still report gender disparities in non-traditional fields. Some studies reveal exclusion of women from specific technical schools in both the Dominican Republic and Paraguay (White et al., as cited in Abadzi 1989) and among rural populations.

10.4   Overall, there is a rich diversity of gender interventions introduced in Bank-assisted projects across all regions (see Appendix Tables 4 & 5). Seventeen completed and 45 recent on-going projects introduced specific interventions. Figure 15 below shows that the most extensively used intervention across all regions (21/62 projects) was expansion of student places in traditional fields for women (i.e., teacher training, nursing, home economics). Expansion of conventional fields was more widespread in many of the MENA and Sub-Saharan African countries where the structure of economy was extensively agrarian, and female participation in the relatively small formal labor market was considerably limited due to traditional and cultural factors.

10.5   General Expansion of Student Places. The most common intervention used to increase female access was the expansion of student places reserved for girls, under the assumption that women would consequently participate in education. Wherever there were no inhibitions for women to join the formal labor market, women have benefitted from the expansion of higher education institutions. In some countries, increases in the supply of places in higher education institutions have contributed to increasing women's access to higher education. However, the degree to which expansion-related policies have increased women's access to higher education varies among countries and regions, depending upon the ease of access of women to the labor market.

10.6   If there are a limited number of student places, many young persons will not be able to attend college. Women are at a particular disadvantage in competing with men for limited student spaces due to negative social and institutional factors affecting their ability to attend higher education. In such cases, it may be sensible to reserve spaces for women when expanding institutions of higher education. In Nepal, for example, two recent projects plan to reserve 10% of the student spaces in the expanding agricultural institutes and the Institute of Engineering for women. Another project in Ethiopia plans to reserve 10% of the seats at the new agricultural department. Reservation of student places may serve an effective intervention to ensure availability of space for women planning on enrolling in particular institutions.

10.7   Another approach would be to decrease the distance to institutes of higher education by extending educational opportunities to the rural and remote areas. Provisions can be made through extension classes or through building new facilities away from the main campuses. A promising project in Tunisia, for example, will establish campuses in different locations in an attempt to expand higher education institutions in remote areas. Recruiting locally is assumed to create an opportunity for women to participate higher education. For example, a Bank-assisted project in Oman will also expand primary teacher training institutes in rural and remote areas. The decentralization of teacher training together with provision of boarding facilities is hoped to ensure increased access for females.

10.8   Traditional vs. Non-Traditional Fields. In countries with more restrictive cultures, traditional fields appear to be more acceptable for women and motivate them to continue their education and enter the labor market.   Therefore, expansion of women's opportunities in these fields in such countries seems to be a rational way of beginning to improve women's access to higher education. Unfortunately, although this approach has increased female participation at the tertiary level, women tend to be concentrated in fields with low rates of return, because wages tend to be low in traditional fields. The expansion of traditional fields in South Asia, East Asia and LAC regions, however, has discouraged women from participating in higher education because these fields failed to provide necessary skills for employment in the growing formal sectors in countries. Certainly, this difference in the expansion of higher education for women between regions reflects not merely cultural differences but also the differences in the demand in the labor market and the size and dynamism of the formal sectors.

10.9   Two examples of promising approaches are in India and the Philippines. Recent projects in India paid particular attention to the fact that higher education institutions for women ought to provide marketable skills to women. The projects have expanded polytechnics for women in non-traditional fields such as computer application, precision instruments and textile design to diversify the curriculum in the new and emerging fields. The preliminary results indicate excess demand for admission into the women's polytechnics. Similarly, a current project in the Philippines is attempting to improve employment and training policies and increase efficiency in the labor market by meeting the skill needs of the labor market, particularly with regard to women, through expansion of vocational training projects. The project supports non-formal, vocational training for women in rural areas and aims to support poverty alleviation by encouraging women to participate in non-traditional fields.

10.10   Interestingly, Sudan is making a major effort to increase women's participation in non-traditional fields and formal labor market to have a fuller participation of women in the development process and overcome projected chronic labor shortages. As women have been almost entirely confined to training in traditional fields such as home economics, nursing and teaching, they are reluctant to seek higher education because it yields few high-paying jobs. The project would increase female access to a variety of occupations at the level of technicians through its support to training facilities, and in turn contribute to the resolution of skill shortages.

10.11   <u>Provision of Single-Sex Higher Education Institutions</u>. Providing separate, single-sex schools in culturally conservative countries where parental attitudes and societal restrictions limit women's participation in co-educational institutions may well increase female participation in higher education. Bank-assisted projects supported single-sex higher education institutions in countries where societal and parental resistance to coeducation exist, alongside private demand for girls' higher education. For instance, a project in Oman would expand girls' access to post-secondary education by providing a primary teacher training college for women. Similarly, a project in Pakistan attempts to increase the supply of primary and middle school teachers, particularly for girls' school in rural areas. Under the project three new female teacher training institutes would be established and seven existing institutes would be reconstructed and expanded to expand female teacher training capacity by fifty percent.

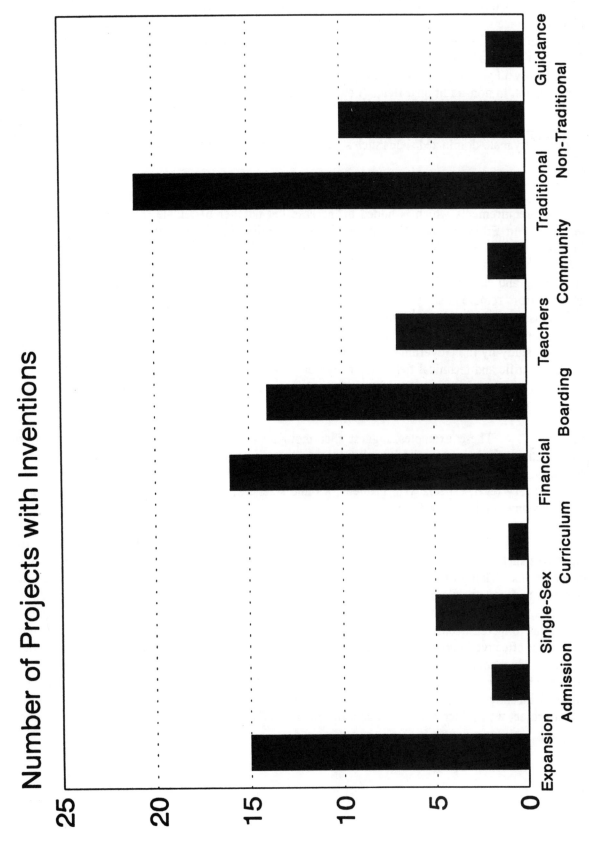

Figure 10. Specific Interventions by Type

10.12   <u>Modification of Admission Criteria for Girls</u>. Women attend poorer-quality schools in disproportionately high numbers. Gender streaming is also evident at the secondary level in many countries since women have restricted access to a broad range curriculum particularly in the sciences and are conditioned by biased learning materials and classroom dynamics (Lee and Lockheed, 1989). Modification of admission criteria for women to facilitate them to join non-traditional fields of study appear only in a few projects, although these measures might be very effective in increasing female participation in non-traditional fields (i.e. science and technology). For instance, an on-going project in the Gambia will establish new admission criterion for primary teacher training institutes to increase women students by 40% by 1996-1997. The goal is to increase the number of female teachers in traditionally male-dominated fields such as science and mathematics to provide role models for school-age girls.

10.13   In Papua New Guinea, a project supports the revision of selection criteria for college entrance requirements which is hoped to increase the number of female trainees in sectors other than teaching. In Ethiopia, the Government plans to modify the admission criteria for teacher training institutes to encourage female candidates. In addition, the Commission of Higher Education plans to reduce constraints hindering entry and enrollment of women in higher education by (i) providing counseling and career information services; and (ii) expanding selected academic programs. In Nepal, students from remote areas have received extra points in the entrance examination for certificated course to increase equality among regions in Nepal. In addition, the Government would introduce a six-month remedial program for students with weak educational background in science, mathematics and language. A recent study by the Government of Zimbabwe concluded that women are likely to remain a minority in all scientific and technical fields for many years, unless some marked changes occur in the country's education and training systems. Thus, the report recommended preferential admissions (quotas) for women entering scientific and technical fields.

10.14   These examples suggest that though used in only a few cases, curriculum reform, modification of admission criteria and quotas do contribute to expanding female enrollments in higher education. However, these interventions will be of little use if women receive poor quality education at the secondary level, especially in mathematics and sciences, as this would negate the beneficial effects of quotas and curriculum reform.

10.15   <u>Provision of Scholarships and Other Financial Assistance</u>. Provision of financial incentives such as financial aid and free tuition, transportation and accommodations are extensively used interventions. Though few projects identified the direct and opportunity costs of higher education as a deterrent to female participation, possibly because higher education is already subsidized for <u>all</u> in many countries, many projects either introduced or mentioned offering scholarships or other financial assistance as a means to increase female participation in higher education. Provision for financial assistance is likely to be most effective in areas where scarce resources of poor families affect parents' abilities to send girls to higher education. For instance, in Indonesia, low female enrollment in the rural areas was found to be due to high direct and opportunity costs of women's education. The Government objective is to create financial incentives to recruit women in rural areas to be candidates for primary teachers. Therefore, a recent project would increase recruitment of female candidates by providing financial aid and dormitory facilities.

10.16   Yet, financial aid, free tuition and boarding have not always been successful in raising women's participation in higher education.[14] Low demand for education even with provisions for scholarships is most evident in socially conservative countries where scholarships encouraged women to travel overseas. One example is a recent Bank-assisted project in Papua New Guinea which envisaged increasing the number of women with graduate degrees by providing overseas scholarships. The project would finance an overseas scholarship program, and special preferences would be given to identify female candidates. However, the preliminary results of the project indicate that there has been low female participation in these programs principally because many women are reluctant to go overseas alone. Thus, provision of financial assistance for foreign education may not be a sufficient intervention where additional cultural barriers inhibit the effectiveness of the scholarships provision involving overseas travel by women.

10.17   However, the same incentives proved beneficial in a culturally less restricted environment. The experience of Indonesia from two Bank-assisted projects appear to be very promising regarding women's participation in the overseas graduate programs. Projects stated that the nomination and selection of candidates for fellowship for overseas training will emphasize increasing the participation of women in the public sector. Preliminary results indicate that female participation approaching the 25 percent target and efforts are being made to further raise female participation.

10.18   Expansion of Boarding Facilities. In increasing student spaces, it is logical to consider the provision for boarding facilities available to women as many colleges are often located in urban areas, especially distant from rural families. Lack of boarding facilities might discourage female participation in higher education proportionally more than for males. Provision of dorm facilities appears promising to increase women's demand for higher education. For instance, expansion of dorm facilities at the agricultural training college in Jamaica increased women's participation more than was expected. According to the project audit report, future provisions for boarding facilities for women would doubtless increase female enrollment given unmet demand for women's training in agriculture. Current projects in India and Yemen recognize this need and provide dorm facilities where distance away from families might be a factor. In a project in Yemen, for example, the provision for culturally appropriate, single-sex hostels is expected to increase female participation by 50 percent at the Faculties of Education (see Box 2).

10.19   Recruitment of Women Faculty. Although there is little empirical evidence to substantiate a link between the number of women faculty and the number of female students at the tertiary level, it has been suggested that lack of women as role models within non-traditional fields may have an influence on the acceptability of women in fields where women have been traditionally under-represented. The lack of female faculty has often resulted in inequality in educational delivery and high dropout rates for women. Recognizing this problem, the University of San'a in Yemen attempted to increase female faculty at the College of Education with some significant success.

10.20   Current projects in India also provide female instructor training institutes for women's polytechnics. Instructor training would be offered for 16 fields in four instructor training institutes. Similarly, a current project in Nepal also recognizes the influence of women faculty on female students and provides fellowships to women candidates with the hope of increasing female faculty in the

---

[14] In India, according to some observers, financial aid did help women enroll in local colleges and universities but not for overseas study. This is yet to be documented empirically.

Box 2: Yemen's Experience in Raising Female Enrollments

A recent project in Yemen proposed to expand women's participation in higher education because of concern for shortages of women teachers and high costs of expatriate teachers. Although the project aimed at increasing educational opportunities at the secondary education level for girls by increasing the female teacher supply, the project introduced policies to improve women's access to higher education.

The project found that cultural factors play a significant role in women's access to education, particularly in the rural areas. The lack of culturally appropriate housing for women at the Faculty of Education also limits women's access to tertiary education. Interestingly, inequality in educational delivery was also noted as one of the obstacles that women confront. Interactions between professors and women students are limited due to cultural factors.

Under this project hostels would be built on three campuses to house approximately 800 female students. Existing hostels facilities in Aden for 240 women students would also be renovated. The provision of dormitories is expected to increase female enrollment at the Faculties of Education by about 50 percent. The stipends provided by the Government must be better targeted to ensure that needed groups such as women and rural teachers are brought into the system. This measure provides for stipends from the Government for all female students while male students receive a targeted financial aid based on their achievement at the secondary education level.

In addition, under the project the Government stressed the importance of women's participation in education and in the labor force by establishing an Advisory Group for Trained Manpower (AGTM). The main purpose of the AGTM would be to review the requirements for trained manpower on an annual basis and to provide direction within tertiary education. Among other things, the AGTM would also adopt or recommend policies to the Cabinet regarding meeting gender needs.

The project diagnosed the constraints on female participation in higher education remarkably well and adopted a "package approach" in providing several measures together, which would significantly contribute to increasing girls' and women's participation in secondary and tertiary education.

---

engineering department. Through raising the quality and number of women faculty in the engineering department, the project hopes to provide role models for engineering students, influencing the acceptability of women in engineering.

10.21   <u>Community Awareness Campaigns</u>.   Evidence suggests that community awareness campaigns are particularly effective at the primary and secondary education level (Herz et al. 1991). However, this intervention has not been tried in many countries in higher education. Only three out of 62 projects with interventions have introduced components for public awareness about women's higher education. Two recent projects in India included a very promising public awareness campaign regarding the programs and the benefits of the girls' education at the tertiary level. This innovative approach used a National Information Center, television and press coverage of the projects and public meetings about the project and programs. In addition, employers were informed about the graduates, providing employment prospects for graduates. Similarly, in Korea public information campaigns were introduced in a leading undergraduate technical institute (Korea Institute of Technology) to overcome the low enrollment of women in institutes focusing on science and engineering. The leading undergraduate university proposed to introduce a program to attract more female students to their campus. Although it is too early to assess this intervention, preliminary results indicate that it has been successful in attracting more female students in science and technology fields.

10.22   <u>Counseling and Guidance</u>. Although the provision of counseling and guidance is mentioned in vague terms in a few projects, introducing programs at the secondary education level may have a positive impact to improve women's access to higher education. Since the early 1970s in many developing countries, admission to higher educational institutions has been generally based on some form of university entrance examination due to an excess private demand for higher education. Provision of counseling and guidance at the secondary level is important to make the best career decision, especially in countries where there are no career information centers and role models are few. Though the projects have not directly supported any interventions regarding counseling and guidance at the secondary level, they pointed out that a number of policies by either government agencies or universities would be introduced.

10.23   Although often a provision for counseling and guidance is suggested in a project, specifics are frequently left unmentioned within the project context. As noted above, however, one particularly impressive project in Korea outlines specific actions to be undertaken in an effort to increase more women in science and engineering fields. To overcome the low female enrollment at the Korea Institute of Technology, the institute itself will introduce the following program to attract more female students: a) The faculty of KIT will visit girls' school to recruit interested women; b) The KIT will send information regarding science and engineering opportunities to the parents and counselors of targeted women; and c) KIT will encourage visits by women students to the campus to learn further of the opportunities available. With the outline of specific counseling and guidance actions to be undertaken, it is expected that more women will become interested in pursuing careers in science and technology.

Quality of Interventions

10.24   In order to get some idea about not only the number of interventions but also the quality of overall effort made in each project to address the gender problem, interventions are rated as follows:

Rating Index	Qualitative Norms of Rating
1	No constraint analysis done; a single, passive intervention was introduced.
2	General expansion of enrollment to meet the (observed) demand in the labor market.
3	Introduced more than one intervention, but not based on a prior analysis of constraints.
4	Introduced a single (specific) intervention based on a prior analysis of constraints.
5	Introduced multiple interventions based on a prior, thorough analysis of constraints.

10.25   The rating index is based on interventions only, and <u>not</u> on the basis of the achieved results from the interventions.[15]

10.26   The number of interventions along with the average quality rating index are shown for each region, and for the country classifications in Table 5. Quite clearly, in terms of both number of interventions and the quality rating index, projects in South Asia appear to be more promising. In East Asia, the number of interventions is small, but the quality is high. In Sub-Saharan Africa and MENA the number of interventions and their quality is much less satisfactory.

10.27   When countries are classified according to the income range, there is not much difference in the number of interventions, but the quality rating index does increase with GNP per capita. However, neither the number of interventions not the quality rating index seem to be related to the structure of the economies as revealed by the proportion of service sector employment, and the proportion of girls in secondary school

10.28   It would be interesting to know whether projects with a high quality rating index were more successful in improving female enrollments that others. Unfortunately, the sample size of these projects with results is so small that no statistical tests are possible. However, preliminary results of the projects with a high quality rating index indicate that the projects with a high quality of index did succeed in improving female enrollment. In comparison, the projects with a low quality rating index failed to improve female participation.

11.   Lessons from Bank Experience

11.1   This section discusses the promising approaches and policy options for increasing female enrollment in higher education. We examine both the projects for which some results are available and on-going projects for which the results are not yet available. Some conclusions about the effective and promising approaches for increasing female enrollment in higher education are given at the end.

11.2   To assess the results of Bank-assisted projects with gender specific interventions, we examined available Project Completion Reports (PCRs) and Project Audit Reports (PARs). Overall, sixty-five projects had PCRs and/or PARs. However, our analysis had to be limited to the seventeen projects that introduced gender specific interventions, because many PCRs and PARs failed to quantitatively <u>measure</u> the impact of the project on women's enrollment rates <u>during</u> and/or following project implementation, even though the appraisal reports included components to overcome gender disparities (see Appendix Table 2).

11.3   Overall, four projects succeeded in meeting the stated gender objectives, five projects were unable to meet stated gender objectives, and four projects partially met gender objectives. On four projects nothing can be said since no measurement of success disaggregated by gender is available.

---

[15] As we already mentioned, the results from many recent projects are not yet known.

Table 5: Qualitative and Quantitative Treatment of Gender-Specific Interventions

	Average No. of Interventions	Average Rating Index
Total	2.15 (62)	2.92 (62)
Regional Variation		
Sub-Saharan Africa	1.7 (14)	2.93 (14)
East Asia	1.9 (16)	3.3 (16)
South Asia	3.6 (8)	4.0 (8)
MENA	2.1 (18)	2.4 (18)
LAC	1.6 (6)	2.0 (6)
Country Socioeconomic Factors		
Income Level Low	2.03 (16)	3.13 (16)
Lower-middle	2.33 (12)	2.79 (12)
Upper-middle	2.17 (3)	3.50 (3)
Employment in Service Sector <0%	2.13 (7)	3.12 (7)
0-0.9%	2.56 (7)	3.14 (7)
15-25%	2.25 (8)	2.84 (8)
>25%	1.75 (2)	3.90 (2)
Female Secondary Enroll. Rate <20%	1.67 (11)	3.00 (11)
20-35%	2.17 (6)	2.80 (6)
>35%	2.08 (6)	3.08 (6)

Notes: Figures in parentheses represent number of projects. The number of interventions is inclusive of interventions such as monitoring, needs assessment and government policies.

Project Results

11.4   <u>Projects Successful in Meeting Gender Objective</u>. Although it is difficult to draw general patterns due to the extremely limited project experience, one thing is clear: demand for skilled women in the labor market was critical for the success of the projects. There seemed to be no strong correlation between the number and type of interventions introduced and the projects' success; the most influential factor among successful projects was a strong derived demand for higher education by women in response to favorable labor market conditions rather than any specific type or number of interventions introduced. This suggests that where a strong demand exists for women with higher educational or technical qualifications, even simple expansion of student places will improve female enrollments.

11.5   This point can best be illustrated by Jordan's First Education Project which expanded student spaces by providing a coeducational Teacher Training Institute (TTI). The results indicated that participation of women has been greater than envisaged. In contrast to the equal proportion of male/female enrollments anticipated for the TTI, the proportion of female trainees increased to about 66 percent in 1978. Opposition against coeducational teacher training among staff and the community were outweighed by the positive reactions of the students and the advantages in the flexibility and variety of the programs. The other projects successful in meeting gender objectives were similarly due to a large extent by the high private demand for higher education among women.

11.6   <u>Projects Which Failed to Meet Gender Objectives</u>. In contrast to the projects for which there was success, among the projects which failed to meet the gender objective the common problem was low demand for tertiary education by women. The reasons for the subdued demand could be many. First, women's entry into the formal labor market is restricted by strong cultural factors (e.g., Yemen). Second, despite favorable demand conditions, parents may be unwilling to send their daughters unless their specific concerns are met by suitable interventions. Third, low participation rates in both primary and secondary education may result in a low demand for higher education (e.g., Pakistan and Morocco). In all these cases, mere expansion will not be very helpful in rasing the level of women's participation in higher education. Focus then ought to shift to the <u>causes</u> of the low demand and introduce appropriate interventions.

11.7   For example, a project in Pakistan expanded spaces in Teacher Training Institutes with the intention of meeting labor market demands for trained teachers; the government could only meet 27 percent of the demand for women teachers. The project constructed three new female teacher training institute (770 enrollment capacity) and expanded student places in seven existing institutes (2,270 enrollment capacity). Upon completion of the new structures and student spaces, it was found that the project facilities were consistently under-utilized and under-enrolled, because the project neglected to evaluate the specific constraints faced by women candidates during their schooling and later in the job market.

11.8   However, mere assessment of constraints alone may not be sufficient to guarantee successful project interventions aimed at increasing women's access to higher education. In a project in Papua New Guinea, for example, the identification of the constraints was based on unsubstantiated theory. When the assumption made proved inaccurate, the project was unable to meet gender objectives.

11.9   In some countries, the demand for higher education places varied according to the available programs. The existence of high female secondary enrollment rates, a high general demand for educated women within labor market, and the availability of student places do not necessarily increase women's access to higher education, unless the educational programs offered to women link to specific demands in the labor market.

11.10   Partially Successful Projects. Four of the 17 projects have partially achieved the objectives set within the appraisal reports. Partial achievement of the goals may be related to the nature and quality of interventions introduced.

11.11   In Kenya, for instance, a Bank project assisted in establishing two agricultural institutes which planned to offer two-year certificate courses in agriculture with a special home economics option for women. Two projects reserved 25 percent of the student places for women. Preliminary results of the project indicated that two institutes were able to expand their enrollment capacity as planned. Surprisingly, upon project completion, one institute experienced a 5 percent improvement in women's enrollment rates over the percent anticipated during project appraisal, while the other institution failed to realize targeted objectives.   The reasons for the shortcoming was cited in the PCR as imperfect advertising and registration procedures at the time the institute was set up.

11.12   Unable to Determine Relative Success. Occasionally, the PCRs do not enable one to determine whether or not the objectives of the SARs were realized.   For instance, a project in Syria supported the establishment of two new Health Technician Institutes in which women were expected to comprise 50 percent of total enrollments. Cultural and social attitudes toward nursing were stated as a major constraints adversely affecting female participation in the nursing programs. Although the project itself did not introduce specific interventions to overcome the constraints identified, it noted that the government should intervene. However, because the PCR mentioned no gender specific outcomes, it is difficult to evaluate the project's impact on women. Interestingly, the Syrian project is not an isolated occurrence as we found four of 17 (23%) of the projects for which gender interventions were introduced and for which PCRs were available had failed to adequately provide measurements to assess the impact of the project on female enrollment rates.

Approaches in the On-Going Projects for Which Results are not Available

11.13   Since the mid-1980s the Bank has paid greater attention to gender issues in higher education projects. Increasing numbers of projects acknowledged gender issues in higher education and a significant number of them introduced interventions to overcome the barriers affecting women's participation in tertiary education.   Many of these projects are recent and the outcomes are not yet available. However, the approaches currently being followed deserve to be discussed.

11.14   Increase the Quality of Education at the Secondary Education Level. It is logical to think that the quality and kind of education received at the secondary level will affect post-secondary educational enrollment. In many developing countries, the irrelevancy and poor quality of educational materials affect girls' enrollment at the primary and secondary levels (Herz, et al. 1991). Therefore, in some cases where quality of basic education is particularly low for girls, improvement of basic educational opportunities (i.e. by increasing opportunities in math and science classes), may ultimately increase women's access to higher education. In fact, many projects addressed the poor quality of female education at the lower levels. In Mali the Government would revise curriculum to emphasize the basics. This would overcome parents' initial reluctance, and is expected to produce more literate and numerate graduates who will be more productive and better able to adapt to the demands of an evolving labor market or continuing into the higher levels.

11.15   A project in China, for example, is focusing on increasing the quality of basic education in order to increase women's access to further educational opportunities. Introduced provisions include: (a) publicity and heightened public awareness of the importance to society of educating girls; (b) strengthening measures to make education compulsory; (c) improving conditions for rural teachers to retain parents' trust to educate their daughters; and (d) targeting provisions of cash to poor families that need to cover school-related expenditures. The project expects a more effective delivery of educational services will result in higher school attendance, higher completion rates and reduce illiteracy rates, thereby increasing the applicant pool for continuing education.

11.16   <u>Increase Flexibility and Diversity and Strengthen Links to the Labor Market</u>. Rigidity in higher education programs has been a particular problem for women, especially for married and/or working women. Flexible programs in tertiary education help to increase women's attendance. Recent projects attempt to raise female participation in higher education through a number of innovative approaches in the design of programs. Short-term and part-time programs, night and weekend classes, and credit systems can enable working and/or married women to attend at a convenient time. The experience in India shows such interventions increased enrollment in higher education among working and married women. In Tunisia, a recent Bank-assisted project which provided short-term courses envisaged an increase in women's demand for tertiary education. The projects in India also introduced flexibility in polytechnics program. Introducing a credit-system allowed women to enter and leave programs.

11.17   Provision of choice in higher education by increasing course offerings can also enable women to choose from a wider range of study, thus helping them tailor their education to private demand. In India, for example, such an intervention was particularly important, for the lack of demand for higher education among women was principally due to limited educational choice.

11.18   Because of the rapidly changing economic structures in developing countries, many countries are experiencing growth in the manufacturing and service sectors. The linkage between women's higher education and employment opportunities may prove important in increasing parental demand for tertiary education for their daughters (see Box 3).

11.19   One current project in the Philippines addresses the employment/education link by encouraging women to enter fields for which demand exists in the labor market. The program encourages women to participate in non-traditional fields and further supports on-going projects to increase female participation in occupations in line with labor force needs. Moreover, to more accurately combine women's employment needs and interests, the project supports funds for a training delivery system which would help meet the training needs of women by supporting communities in identifying training needs for women and introducing matching programs.

11.20   <u>The Package Approach</u>. Preliminary results indicate that where barriers to female access are particularly stringent, multiple interventions may be needed to overcome the constraints. No single measure can resolve persistent socio-cultural constraints affecting women's participation in higher education. Therefore, an increasing number of recent Bank-projects have introduced multiple interventions. For example, a recent project in Nepal is among the best promising projects to improve women's participation in higher education in technical fields. The project identified the barriers affecting women's participation in higher education and introduced multiple interventions to overcome identified constraints (see Box 4).

Box 3: Pacific Countries Study

The Pacific Regional Post-Secondary Education study is one of a series of Pacific Country Studies being undertaken by the World Bank, encompassing Fiji, W. Samoa, Tonga, Kiribati, Solomon Islands and Vanuatu. The project evaluates the islands' institutions of higher education according to their responsiveness to market demands (notably with regard to women). The study's in-depth analysis of the participation of women in post-secondary education is most encouraging. One of the most striking features found regarding the labor force was that over the time period studied, there was a substantial increase of women. Currently, there is a shortage of women in teaching, nursing, business and technology.

In addition to the high demand for educated workers, many of the training facilities experience vacancies (from 27% in nurses training to 42% in professional and teaching areas in institutes of technology), suggesting the need for incentives to increase women applicants. The study highlights the following approaches for increasing female participation in institutes of higher education.

1. Increase scholarships for women: Although currently most Pacific Member Country students receive financial assistance to attend post-secondary education, only 30% of scholarships are allocated to women. Of the four types of scholarships currently offered, only one (Equity and Merit) allocates 50% to women, indicating that access to scholarships is currently skewed against women. The high rate of enrollment in the EM scholarship by women indicates the demand for women's scholarships exist.

2. Increase opportunities for women in high income jobs: An additional approach recommends making conclusive policy to increase the opportunities for women to train for high income jobs. The study found that the most important factor influencing the initiatives by female students was market demand. Interestingly, the demand in the labor market had an even greater influence on student action than parental guidance or counselor suggestions.

Increasing training options within higher paying fields would likely increase incentives for women to invest in higher education.

11.21   Three recent on-going projects in India appear to be among the most promising projects aimed at improving women's access to higher education, for the projects not only expand higher education institutions for women but simultaneously address various constraints restricting women from fully participating in post-secondary education (Box 5: India's Experience). Preliminary results of these projects indicate that the package approach to overcome constraints to women participation is promising. Clearly, some on-going Bank-assisted projects with multiple measures are most to likely increase women's participation in higher education.

Effective Approaches Under Diverse Socio-Economic Settings

11.22   In terms of effective approaches across countries, what broad patterns do these projects suggest? What are the typical constraints affecting women's participation in higher education across countries? Is there any relation between the effective approaches and the stage of country development and/or the nature of the socio-economic setting?

11.23   As noted above, differences in gender disparity are striking when comparing countries within different stages of development. What explains these differences? It is argued in the literature that a decline in the proportion of female participants in secondary and higher education in low-income countries as compared with middle and high-income countries suggests a relationship between women's access to higher education and a country's state of economic development (Verspoor 1990). In other words, economic growth measured by per capita GNP appears to be conducive to development of higher education and increased participation rates for women. Demand for girls' education is estimated to be more elastic than for boys', suggesting that demand for girls' education fluctuates more with the level of national income as contrasted with the more stable and constant demand for education experienced for boys (Schultz 1989).

Box 4: Package Approaches to Overcome the Constraints on Women's Higher Education: Examples from Recent Bank-Assisted Projects

Where barriers to female access to higher education are pervasive, multiple interventions may be needed to increase women's enrollment. The following are examples from a few recent, on-going Bank-assisted projects which adopt a package approach to enhance female enrollment.

<u>Nepal's Agricultural Manpower Development Project (1984)</u>: The project was designed to assist in improving agricultural training at the middle and higher levels. It was already decided that at least 10% student spaces would be reserved for women in middle and higher level agricultural training because the government of Nepal encourages women to actively participate in agricultural and rural development activities. Accordingly, the project introduced gender-specific interventions to increase female participation in agricultural higher education. First, the project would rehabilitate and renovate existing buildings to accommodate 600 agricultural junior technician assistants at two training centers, of which 70 would be reserved for women students. Second, to accommodate students, additional boarding facilities for 180 would be constructed, of which 80 would be for female students. To attract more female students and students from remote and underprivileged hill areas to enroll at Institute of Agriculture, a total of 40 three-year local scholarships would be provided.

<u>Nepal's Engineering Education Project (1989)</u>: The project aims at expanding Institute of Engineering (IOE) to train engineers and technicians in order to alleviate shortages of engineering personnel. Although IOE reserved 10% of student places for women, it had difficulty filling this quota. Of the constraints, lack of programs in which women were interested was cited. The project also identified the lack of appropriate accommodations for women at the IOE as a constraint to enrolling more women.

In addition to reserving seats for women, three additional measures were proposed in the project. First, separate hostel facilities for women would be constructed at each campus. Discussions with female students and female faculty members indicated that the availability of these facilities would encourage more women to enroll in engineering education. Second, two new engineering degree programs would be established under the project in which women were interested, viz electronics and architecture and rural planning. Experience in India, Bangladesh, and other countries in the region suggests that these courses attract women to engineering education. Finally, qualified female faculty would be given preference for the graduate and post-graduate fellowship training program in the project. Raising the qualifications and status of the female faculty is expected to have a positive impact on the acceptability of women in engineering and provide role models to women students.

<u>Indonesia's Primary School Teacher Development Project (1992)</u>: The main purpose of the project is to enhance primary teacher training through a newly developed program at the tertiary level. The program includes addressing the issues adversely affecting women's participation in teacher training programs (which are believed to be principally financial). The government plans to provide financial incentives through provisions of scholarships and boarding facilities. In recruiting the candidates for the scholarship program, preference will be given to women candidates in targeted recruitment areas for teacher training. The selected candidates will receive counseling and tuition support and the program will be evaluated to determine the effectiveness of the scholarships in attracting women. Efforts will be made to retain female participants.

<u>Papua New Guinea's Public Sector Training Project (1990)</u>: In order to increase the percent of female participation in post-secondary education (currently 14% participation rate), the project proposes to offer financial incentives through provisions of overseas scholarships. The project aimed at increasing the number of women in non-traditional fields in particular. To better link employment opportunities and women's education, the project will identify the training needs of women to permit a more effective matching of needs with training opportunities. Through the combined approach of providing scholarships in non-traditional sectors and researching training needs of women, the Papua New Guinea project promises to not only increase women's participation in post-secondary education but to increase participation in areas of high demand.

Box 5: India's Experience in Raising Enrollment: The Package Approach

With the assistance of the Bank, India started an innovative program in 1990 to expand technician education for women through expansion of school places. A number of strategies to overcome various constraints on women's participation in polytechnics were introduced. Apart from expansion of places for women, the following were among the policies introduced to improve women's access to higher education: expansion of hostels, provision for financial aid (by the government), increased link between education and demands of the labor market, introduction of gender neutral curriculum, introduction of public awareness campaigns and flexible programs for continuing education.

Expansion of Places: The projects converted all male polytechnics into coeducational polytechnics and supported establishment of total 19 coeducational and 31 women's polytechnics. Before the projects were implemented, few women enrolled in coeducational programs, preferring instead to enroll in exclusively female institutions. The demand for existing 46 women's polytechnics and coeducational polytechnics was considerably low.

The Role of the Government: Since the beginning of the projects, the government has been very supportive, and perceived the projects as part of the Ten-Year Investment Program (1990-99). A female director who has been very active in women's education was appointed to the Project Implementation Unit. It was also noted that these projects were politically less sensitive because expansion of technician education was viewed as necessary due to a high demand for technician in the changing structure of economy.

Community Awareness Campaign: A large scale community awareness campaign is another significant component of the projects. The National Information Center was established to provide information about the projects and programs. A TV program about the projects was broadcasted on the national TV. In addition, there has been a widespread press coverage about the project, increasing public awareness about the programs. There have been seminars and meetings about the project and programs. To increase employment of female technicians, employers are encouraged to seek women technicians through the communication channel between institutes and employers.

Link to Labor Market: High demand for technicians in emerging fields such as computer applications, textile design, home appliances, precision instruments, and so on existed. However, the existing programs were traditional and did not facilitate the participation of women in modern sector wage employment. An important aspect of the projects is the establishment of a link between the polytechnics and the demands of the labor market. A modified curriculum introducing new programs in emerging fields resulted in an increase in the demand for polytechnic.

Flexibility of the Programs: Previously, rigidity of the programs excluded women who are working, pregnant and/or married. Greater flexibility in carry-over of earned credits enable pregnant women to return to college after delivery and continue education; part-time instructions further facilitated working or married women to participate in these institutions.

Gender Neutral Curriculum: After the project was started, the supervision team found that the curriculum at all levels of education was gender biased. In response, the projects introduced gender neutral curriculum at the technician education level, and encouraged the policy makers to revise the curriculum at the primary and secondary education level as well.

Although it is too early to examine the results of this on-going project, the project design appears to be among the most promising in Bank's projects in women's higher education. Preliminary results indicate that there is an excess demand for enrollment from women for higher education. Only one out of ten women applicants could enter these polytechnics. Why do the projects seem to be so successful in improving women's access to higher education? Apart from the design of the projects, the adoption of multiple measures to improve women's access appears to be an effective policy intervention.

11.24   However, contrary to these propositions, considerable variation in female participation in higher education seems to exist among developing countries <u>with similar levels of development,</u>

suggesting that factors other than income level may influence women's participation. Just as the level of development is an important determinant of the breadth and quality of higher education available (the supply side), the social setting of the country appears to be another important influence on women's demand for higher education. In Table 6, developing countries are classified according to income level (as low, lower middle, an upper-middle income levels according to their per capita GNP) and social setting of the country (ranging from difficult to moderate setting). Factors generating a "difficult" setting in which to improve women's educational participation include: cultural restrictions for female participation in education and in the labor market, dispersed population and low percentage of urbanization, infrastructural bottlenecks, and low levels of female participation in the secondary education. Countries characterized as socially less conservative are those having greater urban population and medium or high levels of enrollment at the secondary level; these are classified under a "moderate" setting. Thus, from the available project experience, a typology of country situations and possible strategies can be delineated to remedy gender gaps in post-secondary enrollment.

11.25   Low Income and Difficult Setting. Available evidence suggests that countries with low levels of income (hence low supply of places) and difficult social settings (with low parental demand for higher education) may have the greatest barriers restricting female participation in higher education. Countries in South Asia such as Pakistan, Nepal, and Bangladesh and much of Sub-Saharan Africa fall into this category. Per capita GNP in these countries is below $500; the demand for women's higher education is very low due to factors such as high direct and opportunity costs, cultural restrictions of women's participation in education and labor force, distance to universities, low level of participation in secondary education and poor quality of secondary education for girls (Herz et al., 1991). These countries experience low overall enrollment rates both at the lower levels and at the tertiary level of education.

11.26   In difficult settings, women's access to any education, and particularly to higher education, is extremely limited, especially in rural areas. For example, in low-income, agrarian economies of Sub-Saharan Africa, women are particularly disadvantaged because they are expected to help considerably on the farm when they continue their secondary education. The effective approach appears to be not only an increase in the supply of student places and single sex institutions, but also introducing policies to increase the private demand for higher education since the house-level constraints have considerable effect on female participation. Despite introducing very gender-specific policies on the supply side, such as reserving student places on single sex institutions for women in some countries, the projects often fail due to difficult socio-economic setting restricting the demand for higher education (e.g. Nepal and Pakistan). In such situations, the only promising approach is to introduce multiple components in the projects, and to encourage women in specific occupations as role models.

11.27   Low Income and Moderate Setting. Countries such as Egypt, India, and Kenya appear to have fewer social constraints inhibiting on women's participation in higher education despite their low level of national income. These countries are socially less conservative, moderately urbanized, have faster growth in their GNP, with medium or high female participation in secondary education. Often the problem in such low income/moderate category countries is the limited supply of school facilities and resources. Therefore, expansion related policies have often been successful in increasing female enrollment rates in higher education. Policies such as increasing student places, reserving places for women, and providing boarding places for girls have successfully increased women's access to higher education.

Table 6: Characteristics of Countries and Promising Approaches: A Typology from Bank Experience[*]

Income Level (GDP/pc)	Social Setting	
	Difficult	Moderate

Low	e.g., Pakistan, Nepal, Bangladesh, Nigeria, Ethiopia
	
	• Expansion of traditional fields (Ethiopia, Laos)
	• Provision of Dorms (Ethiopia, Nepal, Niger)
	• Single-sex schools (Pakistan)
	• Reserving places (Ethiopia, Nepal, Malawi)
	• Establish new criteria for awarding fellowship (Djibouti)
	• Modifying admission criteria (Gambia, Ethiopia)
	• Provide targeted scholarship (Nepal, Indonesia)
	• Provision of overseas scholarships (Indonesia)
	• Introducing new programs with strong demand (Nepal)
	• Provision of counseling and career services (Ethiopia)
	• Monitoring female enrollments (Indonesia, Gambia)
		e.g., Egypt, Kenya, India, Lesotho
		
		• Expansion of female polytechnics (India)
		• Expansion of traditional fields (Kenya)
		• Conversion of all-male polytechnics into coeducational institutions (India)
		• Provision of one polytechnic institute for the handicapped women (India)
		• Public information campaign (India)
		• Introducing gender neutral curriculum (India)
		• Reserving places for women (Kenya)
		• Link to Labor Market (India)
		  - Provision of disciplines in technical fields
		  - Provision of the wide range of disciplines
		  - School-industry partnership to increase employability of women graduates
		  - Examining the utility of technical training
		• Recruit women instructors
		• Provide flexible curriculum
		• Provision of financial incentives (free tuition, transportation and accommodation (India, Kenya)
		• Provision of dorm facilities (Kenya)

Lower Middle	e.g., Yemen, Algeria, Morocco, Papua New Guinea
	
	• Expansion of places (Algeria)
	• Single-sex schools (Yemen)
	• Provision of dorms (Yemen, Algeria, Morocco)
	• Public awareness campaign
	• Provision of stipends[*] (Yemen)
	• Modify admission criteria (PNG)
		e.g., Turkey, Jordan, Tunisia, Bolivia, Philippines
		
		• Expand places (Turkey, Tunisia, Jordan)
		• Provision of coeducational schools (Jordan)
		• Boarding facilities for girls (Jordan)
		• Link to labor market (Turkey, Tunisia, Philippines)
		• Provision of disciplines in technical fields
		• Provision of the wide range of disciplines
		• Improving working conditions
		  - Improved working conditions and career prospects (Jordan)
		  - Give greater responsibility to registered nurses and midwives (Jordan)
		  - Reducing the period of obligated employment to one year for each year training (Jordan)
		  - Provision of attractive salaries
		• Flexible course offerings (Tunisia)
		• Free boarding and lodging for female students (Jordan)
		• Provision of stipends (Jordan)
		• Reduce distance (e.g., establishing campuses in different locations) (Tunisia)

Upper Middle	e.g., Libya, Gabon, Oman, Iraq, Saudi Arabia
	
	• Single-sex schools (Oman)
	• Increase quality at the tertiary level
	• Increase female faculty
	• Provision of boarding facilities (Oman)
	• Provision of training stipends (Oman)
	• Improving working conditions
	  - Provision of attractive salaries (Oman)
	• Decentralize higher education programs (Oman)
		e.g., Portugal, Korea, Hungary, Greece, Brazil, Venezuela
		
		• Expand access
		  - Traditional fields (Portugal, Korea)
		  - Non-traditional fields
		• Increase quality at secondary and tertiary levels (Korea)
		• Link to labor market (Korea)
		• Counseling and guidance (Korea)
		• Monitor and evaluate female enrollment trends
		• Public awareness campaign to encourage female to take courses in science and technology (Korea)

[*]Country examples given are promising interventions directed to improve female higher education in recent and on-going bank projects.
Note: Some of these interventions are introduced by the governments and mentioned in the SARs.

11.28   However, it is also interesting to observe that some of the low income/moderate setting countries have experienced an excess supply of trained personnel in some fields, especially in traditional fields for women, despite a demand for trained workers in non-traditional fields. This is one of the prime reasons of low female participation in technical post-secondary education in India. Establishing a link between labor market and higher education programs, then, is a critical factor in increasing female participation in this category of countries.

11.29   <u>Lower Middle Income and Difficult Setting</u>. Lower middle income countries within a difficult setting share constraints similar to low income countries with difficult setting, the greatest constraint being family or societal restriction. In Yemen, for example, higher education is accessible to students who have a respectable secondary education grade point average. Accordingly, those who qualify academically have access to tertiary education. However, family concern about 'protection' of their daughters has been the main barrier on female participation.

11.30   Interestingly, in these countries, there has been a relatively high demand for educating women in <u>traditional fields</u>. For example, a recent Bank sector report on Yemen found that teaching is increasingly seen as a socially appropriate profession for females. Policy should focus on professions culturally accepted as suitable for females. Projects expanding places for women in such fields as teaching with appropriate housing for women would doubtless expand female participation in higher education. Careful attention needs to be paid to the choice of fields <u>and</u> to culturally accepted modes of housing.

11.31   <u>Lower Middle Income and Moderate Setting</u>. Countries in this category often experience excess demand for higher education by both male and female students as existing higher education institutions are unable to accommodate all students who seek admission. Due to the limited supply of student places, entrance examinations or similar measures are used to determine the qualified students for higher education studies. As such, the constraint affecting women's participation in higher education in these countries comes from the cumulative effects of inequitable access to, and quality of, education at earlier levels. Since female students usually concentrate in non-science and mathematics programs at the secondary education level, access for them to higher education in the fields of science and engineering is particularly limited. Further, the existence of an admission exam appears to negatively affect women because they receive lower resources from their families (than for males) and are therefore less able to compete with the more affluent students preparing through private tutoring to enter the university (Kudat and Abadzi, 1989).

11.32   Turkey, Tunisia, and Jordan are among the countries in this setting where the demand side problem almost does not exist. Limited space is the greatest concern for equal educational opportunity. Since women receive low quality of education at secondary level, they are less able to compete with boys for the limited spaces available in higher education especially in sciences and engineering. Expansion-related policies result in an increase in female enrollment at the tertiary level. In addition, modifying admission criteria and reserving places for girls are promising interventions to increase female participation rates in higher education. Above all, addressing the quality of education and providing counseling and guidance at the secondary level will be imperative to improve women's access to higher education in these countries.

11.33   <u>Upper Middle Income and Difficult Setting</u>. Many oil-producing Arab countries fall in this category. Although they are classified as upper middle income countries, the social setting for female participation in higher education is difficult. Saudi Arabia, and Oman are among these countries.

Women's participation in the labor market is very restricted and concentrated in traditional fields. Accordingly, demand for higher education is also very limited due to factors such as family restrictions on female education. The effective policies seem to be to increase parental demand for their daughters' education. Provision single-sex schools in traditional fields seems to be the most effective strategy. In addition, community awareness campaigns identifying the benefits of female education may increase parental and hence female demand for post-secondary education.

11.34   Upper Middle Income and Moderate Setting. This category enjoys the most gender parity in higher education for all categories. However, women may lag behind men in non-traditional fields in many of countries, such as Greece, Portugal, Korea, and much of LAC region countries. The main constraint here is not the demand for higher education, but the link between higher education that women receive and the labor market. Gender streaming at secondary level is the prime reason for women's inability to gain access to non-traditional fields. Also, in some LAC countries, legal restrictions do not permit women to accept jobs in some professions. Reform of the legal framework and greater emphasis on science and mathematics at the secondary school are critical for overcoming gender streaming in these countries.

CONCLUSIONS AND OPERATIONAL IMPLICATIONS

12.1   Female enrollments, and the gender ratio of enrollments, have improved in all regions since 1970. However, the absolute level of enrollments of both men and women were very low even as of 1988 in Sub-Saharan Africa and South Asia. The low level of female enrollments, and the relatively high dropout rates for girls at the secondary level, are formidable deterrents to expansion of women's enrollments in higher education.

12.2   General expansion of enrollments was the dominating feature of higher education scenario in all regions. A decomposition analysis showed that 70% of the observed change in female enrollments was due to general expansion of places.

12.3   General expansion of higher education may have caused a decline in quality. Notwithstanding the possible decline in quality, the private rates of return are very high for higher education. This may have been an important factor behind the political pressure that led to expansion of universities and colleges. The impressive private rates of return may also have encouraged parents to send their (eligible) daughters for higher education.

12.4   Whatever may have triggered the expansion, the easing of the supply side constraints undoubtedly improved gender parity in enrollments. Policy reforms aimed at contraction of higher education enrollments (to improve quality) ought to consider seriously gender impact to prevent higher education from becoming increasingly a men's privilege.

12.5   The increase in female enrollments conceals the pervasive problem of gender streaming. Women's share in sciences has not improved at all in some countries; even in the developed countries the shares are not high. Clearly this is an area where improvement can be expected only when girls are prepared in mathematics and science courses at the high school level as well as boys. There appears to be a good case for incentives such as scholarships at the secondary school level for eligible girls opting for sciences and mathematics and at the university level.

12.6   Bank project experience on what works to improve female access to tertiary education is so limited that it may be premature to draw firm conclusions. Many of the projects with interesting multiple interventions are currently on-going, thus no results are available.

12.7   Preliminary results suggest that in countries where social factors, including low secondary enrollment rates for women, high direct costs of women's education, and cultural restriction within the labor market, were pervasive multiple interventions are more likely to succeed that single interventions. In addition, even in societies where the formal labor market is growing and few social constraints or qualifications inhibit women's participation, the link between programs offered and the demands in the labor market is critical. High secondary enrollment rates, high private demand for women's education and the availability of student places do not necessarily guarantee an increase in women's participation in higher education unless the programs are dovetailed to meet the specific demands in the labor market. It is not enough to overcome social barriers through policy interventions; future projects need to take an integrated view of the various social _and_ labor market constraints, and include appropriate interventions in the project design.

12.8   The above findings underscore the inherent complexities surrounding women's participation in higher education. These complexities in turn imply that Bank-assisted projects have to pay more detailed attention to specific constraints in different socio-economic settings and introduce suitable interventions. Fortunately, the Bank appears to be moving in a positive direction as a greater number of projects today are introducing specific components in the projects to promote female enrollments than was the case in the 1970s. Of the projects introducing gender-specific interventions in the 1980s, 62 percent were developed during the last five years (1987-1992). A number of recent Bank-assisted projects have multiple, inter-related interventions. Initial project results indicate that this combined or "package approach", well-grounded in country-specific circumstances, may prove to be an effective project design to enhance female participation in higher education as well as to reduce the problem of gender streaming.

12.9   The paucity of the gender disaggregated data on tertiary enrollment rates, as well as secondary school dropout and completion rates, in all regions is a major obstacle to further analysis of female higher education. To facilitate further analysis of the gender issues in higher education, it is of utmost importance to encourage developing countries to collect enrollment, dropout, and completion rates by gender at all levels of education, including higher education.

REFERENCES

Abadzi, H. 1989. "Nonformal Education for Women in Latin America and the Caribbean: Solving the Mystery of the Unreported Trainees." World Bank. PHREE Division. Mimeo.

Eisemon, T.O. 1992. "Lending for Higher Education: An Analysis of World Bank Investment, 1963-1991." World Bank. PHREE Division. Mimeo.

Fredriksen, Birger. 1991. "An Introduction to the Analysis of Student Enrollment and Flows Statistics." World Bank Education and Employment Background Paper Series No. 39. Washington, D.C.: World Bank.

Herz, B., K. Subbarao, M. Habib and L. Raney. 1991. Letting Girls Learn: Promising Approaches in Primary and Secondary Education. World Bank Discussion Paper No. 113. Washington, D.C.

Knight, J. B. and R. H. Sabot, 1990: Education Productivity and Inequality: The East African Natural Experiment. New York: Oxford University Press.

Kudat, A. and H. Abadzi. 1989. "Women's Presence in Arab Higher Education: Linking School, Labor Markets and Social Roles." World Bank. Unpublished paper.

Lee, V. and M. Lockheed. 1989. "The Effects of Single-Sex Schooling on Student Achievement and Attitudes in Nigeria." PHREE Working Papers No. 206. Washington, D.C.: World Bank.

Psacharopoulos, George. 1994. "Returns to Investment in Education - A Global Update." World Development, September 1994, (In press).

Saint, William S. 1993. Universities in Africa - Strategies for Stabilization and Revitalization. World Bank Africa Technical Department Technical Paper Series No. 194. Washington, D.C.

Schultz, T.P. 1989. "Returns to Women's Education." PHRWD Background Paper Series No. 001. Washington, D.C.: World Bank.

Sen, Amartya. 1989. "Women's Survival as a Development Problem." A talk given at the 1700th Stated Meeting of the American Academy of Arts and Sciences on March 8, 1989.

Subbarao, K. and L. Raney, 1992. "Social Gains from Female Education." PRE Working Paper No. 1045. Washington, D.C.: World Bank.

Summers, R. and A. Heston. 1991. "The Penn World Table (Mark 5): An Expanded Set of International Comparisons, 1950-1988," The Quarterly Journal of Economics, XVI:2 (May), 327-368.

Summers, L. 1992. "Investing in All the People: Education Women in Developing Countries." Remarks prepared for a Development Economics Seminar at the 1992 World Bank Annual Meetings.

UNESCO. 1985. "Female Participation in Higher Education - Enrollment Trends, 1975-1982." Division of Statistics on Education, Office of Statistics. Paris.

UNESCO. 1992. Statistical Yearbook.

United Nations. 1981. "United Nations Women's Indicators and Statistics Spreadsheets Database for Microcomputers" (WISTAT), Version 2. New York: United Nations.

Verspoor, A. 1991. "Lending for Learning: Twenty Years of World Bank Support for Basic Education." PHR Working Paper No. 686. Washington, D.C.: World Bank.

World Bank Economic and Social Database (BESD).

World Bank. 1989. Women in Pakistan: An Economic and Social Strategy. Washington, D.C.

World Bank. 1992. World Development Report. New York: Oxford University Press.

Appendix Table 1: Tertiary Enrollment Rates, 1970-1990

Percentage of age group enrolled

	Male							*Female*						
	1970	*1975*	*1980*	*1985*	*1988*	*1989*	*1990*	*1970*	*1975*	*1980*	*1985*	*1988*	*1989*	*1990*
Africa (33):														
Benin	0.25	1.47	2.81	4.55	4.18	4.07		0.02	0.25	0.55	0.83	0.68	0.64	
Botswana	0.00	1.09	2.14	3.11	0.77	0.42		0.00	0.41	0.89	1.20	2.10	2.60	
Burkina Faso	0.06	0.34	0.44	0.94		0.40		0.01	0.08	0.12	0.28		0.30	
Burundi	0.31	0.52	0.71	0.94	1.03	0.93	1.08	0.02	0.06	0.23	0.30	0.36	0.38	0.38
Cameroon	0.91	2.42						0.08	0.40					
Central African Republic		0.67	1.66	2.23	2.40	2.53			0.10	0.14	0.26	0.32	0.46	
Chad	0.03	0.30		0.70				0.00	0.02		0.07			
Congo	3.34	5.05	9.22	11.27	9.94			0.16	0.53	1.52	2.01	1.68		
Cote d'Ivoire	1.69	2.05	4.75	3.99				0.29	0.44	1.00	1.10			
Ethiopia	0.31	0.41	0.71	1.20	1.27	1.33		0.03	0.04	0.13	0.27	0.28	0.30	
Gabon	0.70	2.99	4.04	7.49	6.06			0.12	0.77	1.16	2.78	2.45		
Ghana	1.25	1.79	2.51	2.41	2.41	2.41		0.21	0.33	0.70	0.60	0.60	0.60	
Guinea	1.12	5.50	7.50	3.47	2.31			0.10	1.23	1.81	0.60	0.31		
Kenya			1.47	1.90	2.09	2.20				0.40	0.68	1.00	1.00	
Lesotho	0.59	0.67	1.24	1.26	2.25			0.29	0.44	2.05	1.84	5.56		
Liberia	1.45	2.87	3.65		3.88			0.41	0.86	1.44		1.19		
Madagascar	1.37	1.27	3.07	5.28	4.32	4.16		0.62	1.33	1.47	3.22	3.19	3.16	
Malawi	0.70	0.91	0.97	0.95	1.14			0.29	0.14	0.40	0.35	0.34		
Mali	0.29	1.01	0.50	1.69				0.03	0.11	0.06	0.24			
Mauritania		0.72			6.32				0.07			0.91		
Mauritius	5.23	2.37	1.29	1.30	2.52	2.56		0.25	0.36	0.60	0.75	1.26	1.36	
Mozambique	0.28	0.10	0.15	0.19	0.29			0.21	0.10	0.04	0.06	0.08		
Niger	0.00	0.24	0.48	0.98	1.04	1.22		0.00	0.03	0.12	0.20	0.20	0.21	
Nigeria	0.55	1.32		4.92	4.63			0.09	0.30		1.75	1.80		
Rwanda	0.32	0.58	0.54	0.67	0.73	0.93		0.03	0.06	0.06	0.10	0.19	0.21	
Senegal	2.36	3.21	4.59	3.86	4.61	4.80		0.49	0.73	1.04	1.00	1.20	1.20	
Sierra Leone	0.88	1.13		1.07				0.17	0.21		0.32			
Somalia	0.54	1.04		5.11				0.08	0.12		1.10			
Sudan	2.04	2.54	2.57	2.49		3.40		0.31	0.49	0.97	1.47		2.32	
Swaziland	0.75	3.45	4.73		5.24			0.44	1.51	3.09		3.20		
Tanzania	0.28	0.42	0.45	0.44	0.52			0.05	0.06	0.09	0.07	0.07		
Togo	0.92	2.11	3.68	3.52	4.57			0.12	0.33	0.63	0.70	0.63		
Uganda	0.85	0.94	0.81	1.18	1.40	1.42		0.18	0.20	0.23	0.35	0.54	0.53	
Zaire	1.38	1.81						0.08	0.18					
Zambia	0.68	3.56	2.50	0.88		3.01		0.12	0.57	0.71	0.60		1.11	
Zimbabwe				3.00	8.48						1.46		3.80	
Asia (17):														
Bangladesh	4.05	5.01	5.09	7.96	6.04	5.87	5.37	0.45	0.66	0.87	1.99	1.18	1.16	1.15
Bhutan			0.43							0.13				
China		0.73	1.98	2.24	2.27	2.22			0.37	0.65	1.01	1.20	1.18	
Hong Kong	9.73	14.73	9.38					4.64	5.26	3.57				
India	8.27	8.33	8.00	8.55				2.37	2.78	3.14	3.98			
Indonesia	3.99	3.58	5.46	8.82				1.29	1.37	2.44	4.17			
Korea, Rep.	11.58	15.11	23.56	46.33	49.24	50.35	51.39	3.94	5.35	7.47	21.12	23.17	24.52	25.94
Lao, PDR	0.28	0.45	0.66	2.15	1.91	1.83		0.07	0.18	0.31	1.21	1.03	0.88	
Malaysia			5.40	6.72	7.09	6.60				3.20	5.30	6.18	5.69	

	Percentage of age group enrolled												
	Male							*Female*					
	1970	*1975*	*1980*	*1985*	*1988*	*1989*	*1990*	*1970*	*1975*	*1980*	*1985*	*1988*	*1989*	*1990*
Nepal		2.86	4.19			9.94			0.79	1.12			2.76	
Pakistan	3.49	2.73		6.90	6.70	6.34		1.02	0.91		3.20	3.10	3.10	
Papua New Guinea		3.49	2.83	2.33					1.40	0.89	0.86			
Philippines	17.43		26.80					22.17		28.51				
Singapore	9.32	10.68	9.26					4.13	7.32	6.35				
Sri Lanka	1.33	1.71	3.22	4.54		4.89		1.02	0.96	2.45	3.09		3.50	
Thailand	2.39	4.29						1.67	2.75					
Vietnam		2.57	3.77						1.63	1.02				

Latin America/Caribbean (20):

	1970	*1975*	*1980*	*1985*	*1988*	*1989*	*1990*	*1970*	*1975*	*1980*	*1985*	*1988*	*1989*	*1990*
Argentina	15.74	28.12	27.18	34.14	37.61			12.13	26.20	22.09	38.77	44.07		
Brazil	6.36	10.22	12.32	11.31	10.61	10.60	10.59	3.89	9.22	11.55	11.37	11.20	11.46	11.69
Chile	11.96	17.06	14.93	17.84	19.60			7.51	14.13	11.48	13.87	16.00		
Columbia	6.80	9.92	11.37	12.92	13.18	13.22		2.46	5.59	9.09	12.19	13.52	14.19	
Costa Rica	11.65							9.23						
Dominican Republic	7.09	11.06						5.54	8.90					
Ecuador	10.53		45.22	39.42	34.57			4.61		27.5	25.52	23.32		
El Salvador		10.34	6.12	20.99		19.81			5.26	2.58	15.04		14.40	
Guatemala	5.67	6.47						1.34	1.99					
Haiti		1.04	1.39	1.73					0.32	0.58	0.59			
Honduras		6.18	10.31	11.69		11.76			3.25	6.32	7.20		7.70	
Jamaica				3.90							3.90			
Mexico	9.37	14.68	19.16	19.24	17.81	17.08		2.39	5.56	9.50	11.90	12.60	12.50	
Nicaragua	7.53	10.97	13.03	8.54	7.62			3.51	5.65	11.39	10.98	9.22		
Panama	7.80	17.14	19.36	21.71	18.1			5.85	17.45	24.91	30.05	25.85		
Paraguay	5.03				8.50			3.78				7.40		
Peru	14.77	19.59	24.80					7.95	9.54	13.88				
Trinidad & Tobago	3.70	6.36	5.70	5.76		7.22		1.99	3.85	4.29	3.91		4.80	
Uruguay		17.78	16.30		47.20				14.17	18.80		53.60		
Venezuela	12.85	18.12		30.59	29.00			9.10	15.29		22.06	26.52		

North Africa/Middle East (17):

	1970	*1975*	*1980*	*1985*	*1988*	*1989*	*1990*	*1970*	*1975*	*1980*	*1985*	*1988*	*1989*	*1990*
Afghanistan	0.96	1.72	2.99					0.18	0.29	0.56				
Algeria	3.17	5.79	7.08	9.33	10.70			0.78	1.77	2.66	4.46	5.60		
Egypt	12.00	18.51	23.46	27.39	21.19			4.47	8.33	11.52	12.55	11.73		
Iran	4.53	7.00		6.96	9.43			1.59	2.82		2.68	4.20		
Iraq	7.91	11.80	12.47	15.48	16.77			2.37	6.03	6.07	9.27	10.68		
Jordan	2.88	7.12	16.42	16.81	16.66			1.42	3.89	14.63	15.79	18.24		
Kuwait	3.30	7.13	7.98	14.01	15.74			4.06	11.24	15.01	17.71	20.21		
Lebanon	35.41		47.68	35.86				11.36		22.29	20.35			
Morocco	2.64	5.19	9.31	12.18	13.47	13.15		0.48	1.21	2.80	5.61	7.34	7.68	
Oman		0.06	0.04	1.20	4.78				0.00	0.00	0.79	3.43		
Saudi Arabia	2.99	5.95	8.79	13.50	13.86	15.02		0.30	1.85	5.03	10.52	10.26	11.04	
Syria	14.55	17.52	23.60	22.41	24.82	19.20		3.73	6.34	10.89	12.91	14.48	13.89	
Tunisia	4.64	6.35	7.02	7.16	8.53	9.55	10.13	1.16	2.14	3.08	4.19	5.41	6.18	6.83
Turkey	9.25	14.85	8.93	12.61	14.41	16.25	17.43	2.41	3.14	3.14	6.36	7.88	8.94	9.63
United Arab Emirates			1.65	5.49	4.95	4.76				4.09	15.10	16.94	18.35	
Yemen, AR	0.03	1.27	2.66					0.00	0.10	0.18				
Yemen, PDR	0.10	1.71	2.27	2.99	2.14			0.04	0.42	2.27	2.16	1.54		

Appendix Table 2: Relative Contributions of Expansion, Gender Disparity and Population Composition to Change in Female Enrollment in the 1970s and 1980s

Country	Period of Study	Average Annual Change in Female Enrollment	Proportion Contribution of:		
			Expansion %	Disparity %	Population Composition (Females to Males) %
Benin	1978-89	5.1	133.3	-34.7	1.4
Botswana	1974-84	18.2	56.7	38.8	4.4
Burkina Faso	1970-86	27.1	81.4	18.8	-0.2
Central African Republic	1978-89	12.9	64.3	35.0	0.7
Congo	1974-88	11.6	56.4	44.2	-0.6
Ethiopia	1979-89	10.4	72.9	26.0	1.2
Lesotho	1970-88	21.6	73.8	25.7	0.5
Malawi	1970-88	3.6	75.5	26.9	-2.3
Mali	1974-86	18.2	82.0	17.8	0.2
Niger	1972-89	30.5	59.9	39.9	0.3
Rwanda	1970-80	6.9	79.5	21.9	-1.5
Senegal	1970-89	5.0	81.3	20.3	-1.6
Sudan	1970-87	9.8	28.7	71.4	-0.05
Togo	1970-83	14.5	79.0	21.0	0.0
Uganda	1970-82	6.7	33.8	66.3	-0.1
Average		13.5	70.6	29.3	0.2
Bangladesh	1970-90	6.8	45.3	53.6	1.1
India	1970-86	4.3	32.6	65.2	2.2
Nepal	1976-83	10.7	105.2	0.4	-5.4
Sri Lanka	1970-86	10.8	101.1	-1.2	0.1
Average		8.2	71.1	29.5	-0.5
China	1970-89	11.0	94.9	4.9	0.2
Hong Kong	1970-84	8.4	78.7	23.9	-2.7
Korea, Rep.	1970-91	10.1	83.1	16.2	0.8
Lao, PDR	1979-89	19.6	84.6	15.1	0.3
Malaysia	1979-89	6.7	66.8	26.1	7.2
Singapore	1970.83	8.3	61.6	36.5	2.0
Average		10.7	78.3	20.5	1.3
Argentina	1970-87	8.3	83.8	16.6	-0.5
Columbia	1974-89	7.8	64.4	34.8	0.8
El Salvador	1978-86	46.5	55.9	45.0	-1.0
Mexico	1976-85	9.0	56.6	43.6	-0.2
Panama	1970-88	9.6	79.6	20.1	0.3

Country	Period of Study	Average Annual Change in Female Enrollment	Proportion Contribution of:		
			Expansion %	Disparity %	Population Composition (Females to Males) %
Trinidad & Tobago	1970-86	6.6	85.2	11.6	3.2
Average		14.6	70.9	28.6	0.4
Algeria	1970-88	10.4	68.8	30.1	1.2
Egypt	1970-88	5.8	74.6	23.6	1.8
Iraq	1970-88	9.5	62.4	37.7	-0.1
Jordan	1970-88	16.3	81.6	19.2	-0.8
Kuwait	1970-88	9.9	99.4	9.7	-9.1
Saudi Arabia	1970-86	26.5	56.5	43.0	0.6
Syria	1970-87	8.6	56.8	42.1	1.12
Tunisia	1970-90	9.9	62.0	36.0	2.1
Turkey	1970-90	7.7	61.7	39.2	-0.9
United Arab Emirates	1977-89	26.4	95.9	20.2	-16.2
Average		13.1	72.0	30.1	-2.0

Appendix Table 3: Identified Constraints and Interventions in the Bank's Higher Education Projects to Improve Women's Access to Higher Education

EMENA: 1972-1992

Constraints	Interventions
Constraints Identified in Project SARs:	Interventions Introduced in the Project Design to Overcome Constraints:
• Lack of culturally appropriate housing for women (Yemen 1991)	A. To overcome the constraints identified in the SARs:
• Absence of special programs to recruit female secondary graduates for teacher training (Yemen 1991)	• Provide special hostel for women (build new and renovate existing) (Yemen 1991)
• Inequity in educational delivery (Yemen 1991)	• Intent to target women in stipend provision to provide financial incentives (Yemen 1991)
• Low representation of women in technical fields at secondary level precludes participation in technical fields in higher education (Tunisia 1992)	B. Other interventions introduced in the project SARs:
	• Coordinate government agencies to adopt appropriate policies with the expected benefit of increasing the recruitment of women in teacher training programs (Yemen 1991)
	• Monitor women's needs and make policy recommendations according to needs determined (Yemen 1991)
	• Provide women's teacher training college with boarding facilities (for women) (Oman 1987)
	• Decentralize teacher training program with the expectation of increasing female access (Oman 1987)
	• Government will provide attractive salaries and training stipends for women (Oman 1987)
	• Introduce short-term programs with diverse curriculum (recruit locally) in hopes of attracting more women to technical fields (Tunisia 1992)

Appendix Table 3 (Continued)

South Asia: 1972-1992

Constraints	Interventions
<u>Constraints Identified in Project SARs:</u>	<u>Interventions Introduced in the Project Design to Overcome Constraints:</u>
• Low access to vocational training for women (India 1989, 1990, 1991) • Lack separate residential dormitories for women (India 1990, 1991; Nepal 1989) • Lack of single-sex schools (India 1990, 1991) • Low demand in areas of mechanical and civil engineering (with regard to women) (Nepal 1989)	A. To overcome the constraints identified in the SARs: • Expand women's polytechnic institutes in non-traditional fields (India 1989, 1990, 1991) • Develop and expand degree programs for women in technical fields (India 1991) • Create new advanced fields for women in women's polytechnic (India 1989, 1990) • Reserve space for women in instructor training programs for vocational institutes (India 1989) • Provide short courses in continuing education for women in technical fields (India 1990) • Provide financial incentives: free tuition, transportation and accommodations (India 1990, 1991; Nepal 1989) • Recruit female teachers (India 1990) • Provide scholarships to targeted female students (India 1990, 1991; Nepal 1989) • Introduce new programs in fields in which women seem interested (architecture, electronics, rural planning) (Nepal 1989) B. Other interventions introduced in the project SARs: • Expand student spaces in traditional fields (Pakistan 1977; Bangladesh 1983; India 1972) • Reserve student places for women in non-traditional fields (Nepal 1984, 1989) • Provide scholarships for female students (Nepal 1984)

Appendix Table 3 (Continued)

Africa: 1972-1992

Constraints	Interventions
<u>Constraints Identified in Project SARs:</u>	<u>Interventions Introduced in the Project Design to Overcome Constraints:</u>
• Limited and unequal access to education for women (Niger 1981) • High female drop out rates at secondary and primary levels (i.e, early marriage and parental attitude) (Malawi 1989; Mali 1989)	A. To overcome the constraints identified in the SARs: • Reserve dormitory spaces for women (Niger 1981) • Commission study to observe gender differences in school achievement and factors influencing school absenteeism (Malawi 1989) • Reserve places in teacher training program (Malawi 1989) B. Other interventions introduced in the project SARs: • Reserve places in agricultural institute (Kenya 1978, 1981; Ethiopia 1987) • Monitor and evaluate female enrollment trends and issues regarding women (Gambia 1990; Guinea 1990; Mali 1989) • Establish new admission criteria for primary teacher training (Gambia 1990) • Expand school places in traditional fields for women (Gambia 1990) • Establish new departments in traditional fields for women (Ethiopia 1975) • Government actions: modify admission criteria for teacher training institutes; expand technical and vocational opportunities for women; provide counseling and career services; coordinate women in development programs (Ethiopia 1987) • Provide student dormitories for women (Ethiopia 1987) • Expand non-traditional fields (Sudan 1984) • Establish new criteria for awarding fellowships for women (Djibouti 1989)

Appendix Table 3 (Continued)

East Asia: 1972-1992

Constraints	Interventions
Constraints Identified in Project SARs:	**Interventions Introduced in the Project Design to Overcome Constraints:**
• Parental attitudes against educating girls (Papua New Guinea 1976)	A. To overcome the constraints identified in the SARs:
• Lack of female teachers (Papua New Guinea 1976)	• Revise recruitment procedures for teacher training to encourage representation of female trainees (Papua New Guinea 1976)
• Low female enrollment in non-traditional sectors (engineering and science) (Korea 1989)	• Faculty to visit girls' schools for recruitment purposes (for engineering and sciences) (Korea 1989)
• Hesitancy among females to enter non-traditional sectors (Papua New Guinea 1990; Korea 1991)	• Send information to parents and counselors to increase community awareness of schooling opportunities of girls in non-traditional fields (Korea 1989)
• Low completion rates in primary and secondary level among females (China 1992)	• Special opportunities given to women for (overseas) scholarship program (Papua New Guinea 1990; Indonesia 1992)
• Financial (China 1992; Indonesia 1992)	• Identify training needs of women to permit more effective training opportunities which meet demand and interest (Papua New Guinea 1990; Indonesia 1992)
	• Invite interested girls to visit university campus to increase participation in non-traditional fields (Korea 1989)
	• Conduct study to determine reasons for low participation rates for women (especially rural) (China 1992)
	• Government to provide dormitory facilities (free) (Indonesia 1991)
	B. Other interventions introduced in the project SARs:
	• Expand student places in traditional fields for women (Papua New Guinea 1976)
	• Increase female spaces in non-traditional fields through overall expansion (Lao 1989)
	• Finance student accommodations (Papua New Guinea 1976)
	• Expand educational locations to rural areas to educate rural women (Papua New Guinea 1976)
	• Revise college entrance selection criteria to increase number of women in non-traditional sector (Papua New Guinea 1976)
	• Monitor female enrollment (Indonesia 1985, 1988, 1989; china 1986, 1991; Lao 1989; Philippines 1992)
	• Give equal opportunity to women for overseas fellowships (Indonesia 1985)
	• Reserve percentage of fellowships for women in growing sectors (Indonesia 1989)
	• Give preference to women candidates for teacher training programs (Indonesia 1992)

Appendix Table 3 (Continued)

Latin America 1972-1992

Constraints	Interventions
Identifies Constraints in Project SARs:	Interventions Introduced in the Project Design to Overcome Constraints:
• Most projects cite parity at tertiary level (with the exception of non-traditional fields)	Other interventions introduced in project SARs: • Increase the recruitment of women teachers (Bolivia 1977) • Offer fellowships for curriculum revision affecting women (Bolivia 1977) • Increase enrollment opportunities at traditionally female colleges (nursing) (The Bahamas 1981; East Caribbean 1987) • Expand enrollment opportunities with the expectation that women's enrollment will increase through expansion (The Bahamas 1981) • Government to monitor female enrollment levels in non-traditional sectors (industrial/commerce trade) (Ecuador 1982) • Government will conduct study on training needs of women (Haiti 1985) • Expand enrollment opportunities in non-traditional fields with the anticipation that women's enrollment will increase with expansion (Barbados 1986; East Caribbean 1987)

Appendix Table 4: Results of Bank-Assisted Interventions to Improve Female Higher Education

REGION/PROJECT	INTERVENTIONS	RESULTS
MENA Jordan First Education Project (1972)	Provision of a coeducational teacher training institute to train primary and preparatory teachers, 700 places. Provision of two-year post secondary courses in institutional management and advanced commercial studies in the girls' comprehensive secondary school (CCS), 120 students.	Participation of women in the TTI has been greater than expected. In contrast to the equal proportion of male/female enrollments envisaged for the TTI, which occurred in the first year of operation, the proportion of female trainees increased to about 66% in 1978. Opposition against co-education teacher training among staff and the community were outweighed by the positive reactions of the students and the advantages in the flexibility and variety of the programs. The polytechnic financed by the project is also enrolling female students. In the girls' CCS, the two post-secondary vocational programs (secretarial studies and institutional food and nutrition management) were provided and follow the originally envisaged curricula. The objectives originally envisaged for specific multilateral programs have not been fully applied. Nonetheless, the present curricula allow flexibility and yet retain both academic and vocational programs.
Jordan Third Education Project (1979)	Provision of a community college, which would have programs to train special subject teachers and primary school teachers and technicals. The college would enroll about 1000 students, of whom 600 are expected to be women.	In 1985/86 the college had about 880 students, the majority being women. Enrollment in the following year was expected to reach 1300, exceeding the appraisal estimate by 30%. Thus, both enrollment and graduate output of the college is expected to exceed appraisal estimates. An existing agricultural teacher training institute was to be converted into a prevocational teacher training, increasing the student places from 60 to 256. However, soon after project appraisal, the institution became a community college as part of the Ministry of Education scheme to establish a community college to produce agricultural technicians in addition to preparing prevocational teachers. At project completion, the college enrolled 194 students, including 84 women, a change from the original plan to enroll only men.

Appendix Table 4 (Continued)

REGION/PROJECT	INTERVENTIONS	RESULTS
Morocco Fourth Education Project (1978)	Establishment or expansion of five different post secondary education institutions. All courses and options would be open to women. The institutions assisted under the project and targets are: 1. Regional Technical Teacher Training College. Significant female participation would be in the secretarial option. 2. Two two-year Higher Institutes of Technology. A target female enrollment of 20% of total enrollment has been set. However, this target is unlikely to be met in the first few years of operation because of the present low level participation in similar programs. Boarding facilities for 432 students in each institute would be provided. 3. National Institute of Applied Engineering. A target female enrollment of 20% has been set, but it is also unlikely to be achieved in the first few years of operation. 4. Expansion of Engineering College. The goal for female enrollment is 20% and on current trends this seems feasible. Women comprised 13% of enrollment in 1977/78.	The five higher education institutions assisted under the project have the problems of underenrollment and overly generous space allocation. Although the completion report does not mention participation rate or women in these institutions, the appraisal targets have been too high. The audit reported that most project institutions are still well below targets. Only a third of the target enrollment figures were achieved. The project has contributed to a higher female participation rate by increasing the number of training places in specializations that are considered suitable for female students. The female participation rates in the project's higher education institutions were reported to be between 15% and 20%.
Morocco Fifth Education Project (1982)	Construction and equipping of four secondary teacher training institutes in science and mathematics. 3840 students' places (of which about one-third would be women)	These institutions are underenrolled because only 1870 students enrolled.

Appendix Table 4 (Continued)

REGION/PROJECT	INTERVENTIONS	RESULTS
Portugal Second Education Project (1979)	Establishment of two new home economics programs, reflecting an increasingly important role of women in agriculture. Recruit eight instructors for the home economics programs and provide scholarship for overseas training program of 4-18 months. Provision of the three Engineering Technical Training Institutes. The institutes would have a combined annual output of about 900 (20% women). Equip seven upgraded teacher training institutes. A combined enrollment would be about 2220 (70% women).	Fellowship training was provided for the staff of home economics, among other staff. The enrollment of women in the technical training programs is increasing and has given better opportunities for training to women. The enrollment for Teacher Training Institutes is lower than specific objectives set at appraisal. About 700 students enrolled against an estimated 2220, although it is possible that this would be improved slightly when the new buildings are completed.
Syria Second Education Project (1981)	Establishment of three Intermediate Agricultural Institutes and introduction of home economics and food technology programs. Thirty percent of total enrollment would be women, mainly in home economics (100%) and food technology (50%). Provision of two new Health Institutes (HTI). Total enrollments of the two HTIs would be increased from 300 to 600 (50% women).	Curricula for new specializations (including home economics) were prepared. Staff training (including home economics) was done. The PCR does not include the results of the other objectives regarding women's participation in higher education.
SOUTH ASIA Bangladesh Second Agricultural Training Project (1983)	Improve home economics program of these schools which are for women students by providing 132 man-months of fellowship training for female teaching staff.	None of the fellowships, including fellowships for female instructors in home management, provided by the project were used, mainly due to: (i) procedural delays in obtaining clearances from the National Training Council, which is responsible for approving all foreign training programs for government personnel; and (ii) lack of serious efforts by the Government.

Appendix Table 4 (Continued)

REGION/PROJECT	INTERVENTIONS	RESULTS
Pakistan Third Education Project (1977)	Establishment of 3 new female primary and secondary Teacher Training Institutes; expansion and reconstruction of 7 existing. A 50% expansion in female teacher training capacity is expected. A manpower study of the projected supply and demand for female primary teachers for the period 1977/78 and specific plans for overcoming any imbalance would be submitted to the IDA.	The expansion objective was ultimately achieved. However, project facilities had been consistently underutilized and underenrolled owing to three factors: (i) an over-estimation of teacher demand; (ii) an underestimation of teacher supply; and (iii) an overly rigid application of the quota system which allowed no flexibility for filling seats left vacant by one region with able candidates from another. In 1984/85, enrollments in the female TTI were 76% of appraisal capacity, compared with 93% of capacity in male TTIs. The female TTIs in the rural areas remained the most underenrolled. Maintenance and standards of buildings at TTIs are fairly good. Management and supervision of project generally poor. For example, women's TTI at D.I. Khan was not built according to specification. It had not been visited by any supervision mission. An early draft of the study was submitted to the Coordinating Unit but was found unacceptable. A new report was prepared but the Audit could not find any reference to its being used.

Appendix Table 4 (Continued)

REGION/PROJECT	INTERVENTIONS	RESULTS
SUB-SAHARAN AFRICA Ethiopia Fourth Education Project (1975)	Increase women's participation in higher education by establishing a two-year home economics department. The proposed project department would offer courses in home economics, agriculture, and extension education. Forty students would be trained as technicians, and the training would focus on the development process by developing skills in family care, home management, home crafts and agricultural production.	The project supported the establishment of a Home Economics Department at the Ambo Institute of Agriculture which would intake 40 female students, and this was subsequently constructed. In addition, with the integrated approach to post-secondary education, a further 20 female students have followed an agricultural teacher training course. The audit noted that one point which has not bee given sufficient attention at Appraisal was the impossibility of adding a specialized (and also single-sex oriented) subject to a general course. The solution to the problem, namely a split course between two institutions, was in reality the only way out of such a situation. The transfer of this project item to the Commission for Higher Education also gave rise to difficulties regarding the take up of fellowships. Three fellowships had been foreseen in Home Economics and the Commission for Higher Education selected two female candidates and found places for them in July 1981. However, due to the lack of funds at this late state of the project, the fellowships could not be awarded. The Bank failed to timely explain to the Borrower that fellowships could not be funded late in the Project due to the fact that funds had already been allocated.
The Gambia First Education Project (1978)	Construction of a training center for nurses, an extension to a school of nursing, and two hostels for nurses. Improve post-secondary schools in practical subjects, including home economics; recruit male and female students for nursing training mainly from the rural areas.	The nursing school facilities were ready for operation in their new facilities for the beginning of the 1983-84 school year.

Appendix Table 4 (Continued)

REGION/PROJECT	INTERVENTIONS	RESULTS
Kenya Fourth Education Project (1978)	Expansion of the two agricultural institutes at Embu and Bukara which would offer two-year certificate courses in agriculture with a special home economics option for women. 25% of places would be reserved for women. In 1977/78 each institute had a capacity of 250 students, and the project would assist the Institute in expanding their enrollment up to 400. Construction of a new Animal Health Institute which would have a total capacity of 360 student places, of which 110 (30%) would be reserved for women. Provision of boarding facilities for all students in Agricultural Institutes and Animal Health Institute.	Each of agricultural institutes had its enrollment capacity of 250 expanded to 400, with about 25% reserved for women. In 1986 there were 6,000 applicants, but only 210 were selected, indicating the continuing popularity of the program. New boarding facilities and special courses in home economics were provided. In 1984/85 the Embu Agricultural Institute expanded its enrollment from 250 to 400. Women represent one-third of the enrollment, which is an improvement of more than 5% over the target set at project appraisal. It is clear that the project has fully achieved the planned quantitative objectives. The Animal Health Institute started operating in 1984 with 200 first-year students and is planning to eventually enroll 400 students. About 40 women were enrolled (or 20% of the student population). This is below the original target. However, the authorities see it as a temporary situation due to imperfect advertising and registration procedures at the institute start-up.
Sudan Third Education Project (1984)	Expansion of the Khartoum Polytechnic; program development of the two Teach Training Institutes. The PCR envisaged that the project would allow a greater number of female students to become technicians in various specialties through its support to training facilities. Provision of two man-years of a specialist in educational programs for women in the two teacher training institutes.	In the PCR no reference is made to the impact of the project on women's access to higher education. Twelve man-months technical assistance were spent on women's education in the Ministry of Education.
LAC The Bahamas Vocational and Technical Education Project (1981)	Increase enrollment for the Department of Nursing from 180 to 240 spaces. (Enrollment primarily female.) Project will construct new Hotel Training College for 330FT/100PT students. A large percentage of women are in the hotel/restaurant business (65%); may increase female enrollment.	No specific figures are available disaggregating female enrollment within noted institutions. A donation was made of renovated buildings for the BHTC thereby increasing anticipated capacity for outputs, resulting in an 80% increase in training opportunities. Regarding BSN, there was an actual reduction of training opportunities due to government decree. The government is planning on offering associate degrees at the College of Bahamas. The government plans on merging the two nursing programs to increase quality. No raw numbers are available regarding female enrollment.

Appendix Table 4 (Continued)

REGION/PROJECT	INTERVENTIONS	RESULTS
Bolivia First Education and Vocational Training Project (1977)	Project will offer a four year, post-secondary course to train both basic and intermediate teachers at Warisata Teacher Training College. Current enrollment rate for women is 65%. (Highest percentage of female enrollments in higher education.) Efforts will be made to increase the number of qualified females in the teacher training program. Fellowships will be provided to upgrade curriculum for women's education.	Warisata Teacher Training College enrolled 300 persons (as foreseen) with provision for student housing. According to the report, the new accommodations at WTTC made it possible to achieve planned enrollment. Increase in cost and financial difficulties occurred with WTTC, but the project was implemented despite complications showing the important weight placed on improving teacher training. Male/female ratios were not mentioned, but if the percentage given in the SAR remains valid, one can assume the increase in student places resulted in an increase in female enrollment.
Jamaica Third Education Project (1981)	Within higher education, male and female enrollment rates are about equal. Planned expansion of technical teacher training and within vocational technical institutes. College of Arts, Science and Technology: approximately 575 student places; Technical Teacher Training College: approximately 105 student places (expected 50% female enrollment rate).	Project met most of the physical targets; enrollments at CAST exceeded expectations by 200%. VTDI (instructor training) dropped due to unanticipated drop in demand for technical instructors. HEART found to be on target (Hotel); EPAAs (Agriculture) aimed at producing 1000 men and women annually; 3 years after implementation, enrollment at 31% capacity. Built for 600 students; 500 men (residential) and 100 women (non-residential). Low male enrollment rate due to uncertainty of employment in the agricultural sector, low career security and limited possibilities for advancement within agricultural sector. Noted within report: increasing residential options for women would most likely increase female enrollment. Currently 38% female enrollment rate; residence halls–16.6% for females. PAR assessed problem to be low male enrollment rate.
ASIA Indonesia First Teacher Training Project (1977)	Project will expand enrollment places for primary teacher training (grades 10-12) by 7000 (57% women).	Trained 6100 teachers. PCR does not provide statistics regarding female enrollment rates. No gender-specific results provided. Therefore, it is difficult to determine the success or failure of the project.

Appendix Table 4 (Continued)

REGION/PROJECT	INTERVENTIONS	RESULTS
Papua New Guinea First Education Project (1976)	Increase student places in Madang Teachers College by 144 (2/3 women), finance student accommodations at Madang. focus on increasing the number of female teachers. Highland Agricultural Training Institute will begin training females in agriculture through and extension program. Will increase these spaces from 60 to 200. Home economics will be taught through this program as well. The government will revise selection criteria for college entrance requirements to increase the number of females in non-traditional sectors. Also, will revise recruitment procedures for primary teacher training to encourage female representation in less developed areas. Groka Teachers College (secondary teacher training) expected to increase enrollment to 630 (30% women). In Allied Health Sciences, goal is to increase enrollment from 120 to 165 (female enrollment rate expected to expand with overall enrollment increases).	Within agriculture sector (Highland Agricultural Institute) female enrollments rates fell 50% short of targets: 120 female enrollment (30% expected). Suggested reasons for not meeting target: (i) unqualified applicant pool; (ii) small demand for women with agricultural training; (iii) belief that farming is done mainly by women found to be unjustified. College of Allied Health Sciences anticipated an increase in the female enrollment rate to 30% (overall enrollment dropped from 120 to 117). Female enrollment remained constant (12-16%). Female enrollment at Madang (Primary Teacher Training College) also fell below target. Female enrollment actually fell between 1977 (42%) and 1982 (33%), well below project target of 50%. Reasons for not meeting targets: (i) appeal of other tertiary programs (competing with teachers colleges); (ii) secondary school graduates chose direct employment; (iii) small pool of qualified applicants; (iv) social attitudes towards female enrollment at high levels of education prohibitive. Groka's Teacher Training College (secondary) also fell below expansion target (from 430 to 630 student places). The average enrollment rate was only 70% of capacity between 1980-82 (30% women). In recent years the college has been attracting a greater proportion of women than men. Reasons for underenrollment same as for primary teacher training.

Appendix Table 5: Recent and On-Going Bank-Assisted Interventions to Improve Female Access to Higher Education

Project/Country	Type	Establish campus/expand places	Modify admissions criteria	Provide single-sex schools	Curriculum reform	Providing scholarship/other financial aid	Provide boarding facilities	Recruit women teachers	Evaluate needs of women	Community awareness campaign	Expand places in traditional fields	Provide programs for women in growing sectors	Provide counseling and guidance	Monitor project results	Other policies (Gov't policies)
SUB-SAHARAN AFRICA															
Djibouti Manpower and Education Development (1989)	Univ.					XX									
Ethiopia Fourth Education (1975)	Voc.														
Ethiopia Sixth Education (1984)	T.T.	XX													
Ethiopia Seventh Education (1987)	Voc.						XX					XX			XX
Gambia Education (1990)	T.T.		XX								XX			XX	
Guinea Education Sector Adjustment (1990)	Univ.								XX		XX				
Kenya Fourth Education (1978)	Tech.														
Kenya Fifth Education (1981)	Tech.					XX	XX					XX			
Kenya Universities Investment (1981)	Univ.													XX	
Kenya Education Sector Adjustment Program (1991)	Univ.													XX	
Malawi Second Education Sector Credit (1989)	Univ.								XX		XX				
Mali Education Sector Consolidation (1989)	Univ.								XX					XX	
Niger Education (1981)	Tech.	XX					XX								
Sudan Third Education (1984)	Tech.	XX													
SOUTH ASIA															
Bangladesh Second Agricultural Training (1983)	Voc./Tech.							XX							

Appendix **Table 5** (Continued)

Project/Country	Type	Establish campus/ expand places	Modify admissions criteria	Provide single-sex schools	Curriculum reform	Providing scholarship/ other financial aid	Provide boarding facilities	Recruit women teachers	Evaluate needs of women	Community awareness campaign	Expand places in traditional fields	Provide programs for women in growing sectors	Provide counseling and guidance	Monitor project results	Other policies (Gov't policies)
India Education (1972)	Voc.										XX				
India Vocational Training (1989)	Tech.			XX				XX	XX	XX		XX			
India Technical Education (1990)	Tech.	XX		XX		XX	XX	XX	XX			XX			XX
India Second Technical Education (1991)	Tech.			XX		XX	XX					XX			
Nepal Agricultural Manpower Development (1984)	Tech.					XX	XX					XX			
Nepal Engineering Education (1989)	Univ.					XX	XX	XX				XX			
Pakistan Third Education (1977)	T.T.			XX			XX		XX		XX				
MENA Algeria Fourth Education (1978)	T.T./ Tech.	XX				XX	XX								
Jordan First Education (1972)	T.T./ Tech.										XX				
Jordan Third Education (1979)	T.T./ Tech.										XX				
Jordan Fourth Education (1981)	Voc./ Tech.	XX				XX	XX				XX			XX	
Jordan First Manpower Development (1985)	Voc.						XX				XX				XX
Morocco Fifth Education (1982)	T.T.										XX				
Morocco Fourth Education (1978)	T.T./ Tech.	XX					XX								
Oman Second Education (1984)	Univ.														XX

Appendix Table 5 (Continued)

Project/Country	Type	Establish campus/ expand places	Modify admissions criteria	Provide single-sex schools	Curriculum reform	Providing scholarship/ other financial aid	Provide boarding facilities	Recruit women teachers	Evaluate needs of women	Community awareness campaign	Expand places in traditional fields	Provide programs for women in growing sectors	Provide counseling and guidance	Monitor project results	Other policies (Gov't policies)
Oman Third Education (1987)	T.T.						XX				XX				XX
Portugal Education (1978)	T.T.										XX				
Portugal Second Education (1979)	Voc./ Tech.					XX		XX			XX	XX			
Syria Education (1977)	T.T.										XX				
Syria Second Education (1981)	Voc.										XX				XX
Tunisia Fifth Education (1982)	T.T./ Tech.										XX				
Tunisia Higher Education Restructuring (1992)	Univ.	XX										XX			
Turkey Second Industrial Training (1988)	Voc.	XX									XX				
Yemen Technical Training (1985)	Tech.	XX													
Yemen Secondary Teacher Training (1991)	T.T.	XX				XX	XX		XX						XX
EAST ASIA China Second Agricultural Education (1984)	Voc.	XX													
China Education Development in Poor Provinces (1992)	Tech.								XX					XX	
China Key Studies Development (1991)	Tech.												XX	XX	
China Provincial Universities (1986)	Univ.													XX	
Indonesia Higher Education Development (1988)	Univ.													XX	

Appendix Table 5 (Continued)

Project/Country	Type	Establish campus/ expand places	Modify admissions criteria	Provide single-sex schools	Curriculum reform	Providing scholarship/ other financial aid	Provide boarding facilities	Recruit women teachers	Evaluate needs of women	Community awareness campaign	Expand places in traditional fields	Provide programs for women in growing sectors	Provide counseling and guidance	Monitor project results	Other policies (Gov't policies)
Indonesia Primary School Teacher Development (1992)	T.T.					XX			XX						
Indonesia Professional Human Resources Development (1989)	Voc.					XX			XX					XX	
Indonesia Science and Technical Training (1985)	Tech.					XX									
Indonesia Second University Development (1985)	Univ.													XX	
Indonesia Second Higher Education Development (1991)	Univ.													XX	
Korea Technology Advancement (1989)	Tech.									XX			XX		
Lao National Polytechnic Institute (1989)	Tech.	XX							XX					XX	
Malaysia University Development	Univ.													XX	
Papua New Guinea First Education (1976)	Univ.	XX	XX			XX		XX			XX				
Papua New Guinea Public Sector Training (1990)	Tech.					XX			XX					XX	
Philippines Second Vocation Training (1992)	Voc.								XX					XX	
LAC Bahamas Vocational and Technical Training (1981)	Voc./Tech.										XX				
Barbados Second Education and Training (1986)	Voc./Tech.	XX													

Appendix Table 5 (Continued)

Project/Country	Type	Establish campus/ expand places	Modify admissions criteria	Provide single-sex schools	Curriculum reform	Providing scholarship/ other financial aid	Provide boarding facilities	Recruit women teachers	Evaluate needs of women	Community awareness campaign	Expand places in traditional fields	Provide programs for women in growing sectors	Provide counseling and guidance	Monitor project results	Other policies (Gov't policies)
Bolivia Education and Vocational Training (1977)	T.T.				XX	XX		XX							
Eastern Caribbean Fourth Development Bank Regional Vocational and Technical Education (1987)	Tech./ Voc.										XX	XX			
Ecuador Second Vocational Training (1982)	Voc.								XX					XX	
Haiti Fourth Education and Training (1985)	T.T.								XX						

Distributors of World Bank Publications

ARGENTINA
Carlos Hirsch, SRL
Galeria Guemes
Florida 165, 4th Floor-Ofc. 453/465
1333 Buenos Aires

**AUSTRALIA, PAPUA NEW GUINEA,
FIJI, SOLOMON ISLANDS,
VANUATU, AND WESTERN SAMOA**
D.A. Information Services
648 Whitehorse Road
Mitcham 3132
Victoria

AUSTRIA
Gerold and Co.
Graben 31
A-1011 Wien

BANGLADESH
Micro Industries Development
Assistance Society (MIDAS)
House 5, Road 16
Dhanmondi R/Area
Dhaka 1209

Branch offices:
Pine View, 1st Floor
100 Agrabad Commercial Area
Chittagong 4100

BELGIUM
Jean De Lannoy
Av. du Roi 202
1060 Brussels

CANADA
Le Diffuseur
151A Boul. de Mortagne
Boucherville, Québec
J4B 5E6

Renouf Publishing Co.
1294 Algoma Road
Ottawa, Ontario
K1B 3W8

CHILE
Invertec IGT S.A.
Av. Santa Maria 6400
Edificio INTEC, Of. 201
Santiago

CHINA
China Financial & Economic
Publishing House
8, Da Fo Si Dong Jie
Beijing

COLOMBIA
Infoenlace Ltda.
Apartado Aereo 34270
Bogota D.E.

COTE D'IVOIRE
Centre d'Edition et de Diffusion
Africaines (CEDA)
04 B.P. 541
Abidjan 04 Plateau

CYPRUS
Center of Applied Research
Cyprus College
6, Diogenes Street, Engomi
P.O. Box 2006
Nicosia

DENMARK
SamfundsLitteratur
Rosenoerns Allé 11
DK-1970 Frederiksberg C

DOMINICAN REPUBLIC
Editora Taller, C. por A.
Restauración e Isabel la Católica 309
Apartado de Correos 2190 Z-1
Santo Domingo

EGYPT, ARAB REPUBLIC OF
Al Ahram
Al Galaa Street
Cairo

The Middle East Observer
41, Sherif Street
Cairo

FINLAND
Akateeminen Kirjakauppa
P.O. Box 128
SF-00101 Helsinki 10

FRANCE
World Bank Publications
66, avenue d'Iéna
75116 Paris

GERMANY
UNO-Verlag
Poppelsdorfer Allee 55
D-5300 Bonn 1

HONG KONG, MACAO
Asia 2000 Ltd.
46-48 Wyndham Street
Winning Centre
2nd Floor
Central Hong Kong

HUNGARY
Foundation for Market Economy
Dombovari Ut 17-19
H-1117 Budapest

INDIA
Allied Publishers Private Ltd.
751 Mount Road
Madras - 600 002

Branch offices:
15 J.N. Heredia Marg
Ballard Estate
Bombay - 400 038

13/14 Asaf Ali Road
New Delhi - 110 002

17 Chittaranjan Avenue
Calcutta - 700 072

Jayadeva Hostel Building
5th Main Road, Gandhinagar
Bangalore - 560 009

3-5-1129 Kachiguda
Cross Road
Hyderabad - 500 027

Prarthana Flats, 2nd Floor
Near Thakore Baug, Navrangpura
Ahmedabad - 380 009

Patiala House
16-A Ashok Marg
Lucknow - 226 001

Central Bazaar Road
60 Bajaj Nagar
Nagpur 440 010

INDONESIA
Pt. Indira Limited
Jalan Borobudur 20
P.O. Box 181
Jakarta 10320

IRAN
Kowkab Publishers
P.O. Box 19575-511
Tehran

IRELAND
Government Supplies Agency
4-5 Harcourt Road
Dublin 2

ISRAEL
Yozmot Literature Ltd.
P.O. Box 56055
Tel Aviv 61560

ITALY
Licosa Commissionaria Sansoni SPA
Via Duca Di Calabria, 1/1
Casella Postale 552
50125 Firenze

JAPAN
Eastern Book Service
Hongo 3-Chome, Bunkyo-ku 113
Tokyo

KENYA
Africa Book Service (E.A.) Ltd.
Quaran House, Mfangano Street
P.O. Box 45245
Nairobi

KOREA, REPUBLIC OF
Pan Korea Book Corporation
P.O. Box 101, Kwangwhamun
Seoul

Korean Stock Book Centre
P.O. Box 34
Yeoeido
Seoul

MALAYSIA
University of Malaya Cooperative
Bookshop, Limited
P.O. Box 1127, Jalan Pantai Baru
59700 Kuala Lumpur

MEXICO
INFOTEC
Apartado Postal 22-860
14060 Tlalpan, Mexico D.F.

NETHERLANDS
De Lindeboom/InOr-Publikaties
P.O. Box 202
7480 AE Haaksbergen

NEW ZEALAND
EBSCO NZ Ltd.
Private Mail Bag 99914
New Market
Auckland

NIGERIA
University Press Limited
Three Crowns Building Jericho
Private Mail Bag 5095
Ibadan

NORWAY
Narvesen Information Center
Book Department
P.O. Box 6125 Etterstad
N-0602 Oslo 6

PAKISTAN
Mirza Book Agency
65, Shahrah-e-Quaid-e-Azam
P.O. Box No. 729
Lahore 54000

PERU
Editorial Desarrollo SA
Apartado 3824
Lima 1

PHILIPPINES
International Book Center
Suite 1703, Cityland 10
Condominium Tower 1
Ayala Avenue, H.V. dela
Costa Extension
Makati, Metro Manila

POLAND
International Publishing Service
UL. Piekna 31/37
00-677 Warzawa

For subscription orders:
IPS Journals
UL. Okrezna 3
02-916 Warszawa

PORTUGAL
Livraria Portugal
Rua Do Carmo 70-74
1200 Lisbon

SAUDI ARABIA, QATAR
Jarir Book Store
P.O. Box 3196
Riyadh 11471

**SINGAPORE, TAIWAN,
MYANMAR, BRUNEI**
Gower Asia Pacific Pte Ltd.
Golden Wheel Building
41, Kallang Pudding, #04-03
Singapore 1334

SOUTH AFRICA, BOTSWANA
For single titles:
Oxford University Press
Southern Africa
P.O. Box 1141
Cape Town 8000

For subscription orders:
International Subscription Service
P.O. Box 41095
Craighall
Johannesburg 2024

SPAIN
Mundi-Prensa Libros, S.A.
Castello 37
28001 Madrid

Librería Internacional AEDOS
Consell de Cent, 391
08009 Barcelona

SRI LANKA AND THE MALDIVES
Lake House Bookshop
P.O. Box 244
100, Sir Chittampalam A.
Gardiner Mawatha
Colombo 2

SWEDEN
For single titles:
Fritzes Fackboksforetaget
Regeringsgatan 12, Box 16356
S-103 27 Stockholm

For subscription orders:
Wennergren-Williams AB
P. O. Box 1305
S-171 25 Solna

SWITZERLAND
For single titles:
Librairie Payot
Case postale 3212
CH 1002 Lausanne

For subscription orders:
Librairie Payot
Service des Abonnements
Case postale 3312
CH 1002 Lausanne

THAILAND
Central Department Store
306 Silom Road
Bangkok

**TRINIDAD & TOBAGO, ANTIGUA
BARBUDA, BARBADOS,
DOMINICA, GRENADA, GUYANA,
JAMAICA, MONTSERRAT, ST.
KITTS & NEVIS, ST. LUCIA,
ST. VINCENT & GRENADINES**
Systematics Studies Unit
#9 Watts Street
Curepe
Trinidad, West Indies

UNITED KINGDOM
Microinfo Ltd.
P.O. Box 3
Alton, Hampshire GU34 2PG
England